GOOD·OLD·DAYS®

Saturdays
in the
Good Old Days™

Edited by Ken and Janice Tate

HOUSE of
WHITE
BIRCHES
PUBLISHERS
SINCE 1947

Saturdays in the Good Old Days™

Editors: Ken and Janice Tate
Managing Editor: Barb Sprunger
Editorial Assistant: Joanne Neuenschwander
Copy Supervisor: Michelle Beck
Copy Editors: Läna Schurb, Judy Weatherford

Publishing Services Director: Brenda Gallmeyer
Art Director: Brad Snow
Assistant Art Director: Nick Pierce
Graphic Arts Supervisor: Ronda Bechinski
Production Artists: Nicole Gage, Janice Tate
Production Assistants: Marj Morgan, Jessica Tate
Photography Supervisor: Tammy Christian
Photography: Don Clark, Matthew Owen
Photo Stylists: Tammy M. Smith, Tammy Steiner

Chief Executive Officer: David McKee
Marketing Director: Dan Fink

Printed in China
First Printing: 2007
Library of Congress Number: 2006926373
ISBN: 978-1-59217-140-8
Good Old Days Customer Service: (800) 829-5865

1 2 3 4 5 6 7 8 9

Dear Friends of the Good Old Days,

Decades ago when my dear wife, Janice, and I were courting, I liked to take her to a Saturday night picture show at the Owen Theatre in Branson, Mo. Like so many other young folks, we liked to stop off at the soda fountain before the show (it was always closed afterwards).

Our soda fountain was located in the Alexander Drug Store—one of countless similar establishments across the country that doled out sweet ice cream sodas or soft drinks mixed right there before your thirsty eyes. There was nothing quite like sharing a soda with your best girl on a Saturday night.

Ah, those Saturdays in the Good Old Days! Remembering them for me is a lot like going on a quick trip back to the days the Alexander Drug Store.

Out in front there hung a sign: "Come On In, It's Cool Inside!" It was one of the first establishments in town to get air conditioning. What a delightful way to change a hot, sultry Saturday afternoon into a cool oasis.

Saturdays were always entertaining. Whether it was a movie for us kids, shopping for Mama or Daddy's favorite—just sitting on the bench on the town square whittling and jawing with the menfolk—it was always fun.

Just like Alexander's soda fountain and its candy counter, there was an inherent sweetness about those Saturdays in the Good Old Days. The drug store had the traditional fountain with stools (usually lined with youthful patrons) and a booth section with two or three tables.

When I was young, I thought the drug store was huge. Years later, on a trip back home to visit my parents, Janice and I returned to that same drug store. It wasn't as cavernous as I remembered it.

There was still a soda fountain; modernized, but still there. About 20 years ago I returned again to find that it had been replaced by a delicatessen.

Today I miss those deliciously sweet Saturdays that filled my hometown. One of my favorite memories is of taking our son to the same candy counter at the old drug store and seeing his eyes light up with the sweet possibilities that a dime could bring. Yes, those Saturdays of old were both sweet *and* entertaining!

Janice and I hope that you find this book a lot like stepping back to those Saturdays at the movie theatre and the soda fountain. We hope that inside you'll find plenty to entertain you from those days gone by. We know you will find something sweet—maybe even bittersweet at times.

Saturdays in the Good Old Days were a great time to be a kid! Come on inside the pages of this book and you'll see. Or, like the sign in front of the Alexander Drug Store said, "Come On In, It's Cool Inside!"

Ken Tate

❧ Contents ❧

Matinee Magic • 6

Town Days • 34

Saturday Adventures • 68

Saturday Night Revelry • 100

Wonderful Sundays • 130

Matinee Magic

Chapter One

My greatest curse was also one of my greatest blessings when I was growing up back in the Good Old Days. You see, I came from a long line of short men. Grandpa Tate probably was about five feet, six inches, and Daddy was maybe an inch or two taller than Grandpa.

That genetic, biological fact was compounded by being one of the youngest in my class in my small rural school in the hills of southern Missouri.

So I was, perpetually, the shortest boy in the classroom, and on the playground, basketball court and baseball diamond.

People constantly guessed me to be younger than I really was. And I *hated* that!

Howard Gossage once philosophized, "If you have a lemon, make lemonade!" I guess I came to that conclusion without even knowing who Howard Gossage was, because about the time I turned 13, I found a reason to make the bitter taste of being short a lot sweeter.

I had a *Grit* newspaper route that took me to Branson, the nearest town of any size, every Saturday morning. I rode in with Daddy as he headed for the lumber yard that was his six-day-a-week job, arriving about 7 a.m.

After a grueling morning and early afternoon of walking several miles to homes and businesses and delivering over 100 of the weekly papers, I was able to relax with a chocolate soda or a malt at Alexander's Drug on Commercial street.

Then came my favorite time of the week: the matinee magic at the Owen Theatre.

The box office opened around 1:30 p.m., and the show started promptly at 2 p.m. I don't remember the order exactly, but I know there was a couple of cartoons, a serial and usually a newsreel thrown in before the main feature.

If we kids were really lucky, there was a double feature. When that happened, I was able to immerse myself in the magic of the theater until it was time for Daddy to get off work and head home.

I remember the Saturday after I turned 13 years old. I was dreading it. Matinee seats at the theatre went for a dime for those who were 12 and under. But for old-timers like I had just become, the price jumped to 15 cents.

> ## *I guess they thought we teenagers were made of money!*

I guess they thought we teenagers were made of money.

I stood in line with the usual bunch of moviegoers, lost between the "little kids" who were my size or shorter and those of about my age who towered over me. When I reached the ticket window, the lady scarcely looked at me.

"That'll be a dime," she intoned. I didn't correct her.

Suddenly, being short took on a whole new meaning. So what if others were taller? My size just moved a nickel from the admission price to the concession stand! I milked my height advantage until I was at the end of my freshman year of high school and headed to 15. That's when a growth spurt ended all doubt about what price I should be paying.

It is ironic when I see youngsters today who are in such a hurry to grow up, and I reflect on all of the nickels I saved by appearing to be younger than I really was. It made my matinee magic lemonade all the sweeter back in the Good Old Days.

—Ken Tate

Facing page: *Saturday Afternoon at the Movies* by Lee Dubin, Courtesy of Wild Wings

The 35-Cent Babysitter

By James D. Doggette Jr.

When I was a kid growing up in New Orleans during the early 1950s, one of the excursions I looked forward to most was going to the local movie theater on Saturdays.

We hit the streets of our neighborhood after breakfast to meet up with our friends. It wasn't long before the conversation turned to the afternoon triple-feature matinee and how we could obtain 25 cents for admission.

We bounced ideas off one another as we played pitch-and-catch in the street. Barely minutes passed before we had the answer. My sister, the two girls next door and their friend from across the street broke out that sidewalk Kool-Aid stand with whirlwind precision.

My friend Morris and I took off on our bikes in one direction; my brother and his friend Larry took off in another. We combed the city streets for blocks, looking for discarded pop bottles. We even asked people sitting on their front porches or in their yards if they had empty soda bottles we could have.

We'd bring them home and clean them up with the garden hose, then bring them down to the corner store to get the 1-cent deposit on each bottle.

This endeavor would usually bring in only a little more than half of the amount needed, however. By midmorning, it was obvious that if we were going to make it, we would have to trick our parents into giving us odd jobs to earn the rest. Our parents would gleefully respond, giving us such chores as weeding the victory garden, shining their shoes and picking up trash.

The door to the movie house opened at 11:45 a.m. At just about that time, we were crossing St. Claude Avenue hand-in-hand, opposite the theater, each with 35 cents. After paying a quarter for an admission ticket, we would head to the snack bar. After spending 5 cents on a large box of popcorn and another nickel on a big, ice-cold soda, we went and found our seats.

"I had some of the best naps in the world with that 35-cent babysitter."

After just a few minutes the lights lowered and the picture began as the curtain was drawn back, revealing the screen. The show started with previews—the world newsreel, a cartoon or two, and then the first movie. Then came more cartoons and the other two features.

The matinee let out around 5:45 p.m. We walked home, talking about the great entertainment we had enjoyed and thinking about the "fast one" we had pulled on our parents.

Little did I realize, until I was a grown man with a family of my own, that the joke had been on us. While talking with my mother one day, I casually mentioned the escapade. She smiled sweetly. "Son, I taught you the value of money, and had some of the best naps in the world with that 35-cent baby sitter." My mouth dropped wide open. We'd been had.

With eyes glittering lovingly, she reached across the table and softly patted my cheek as she blew me a kiss. I started smiling, and then broke into laughter. ❖

Backstage At the Palace

By Winnie Schuetz

One night, as I watched an old movie on television, a familiar little woman appeared on the screen. I sat mesmerized as I recognized someone I had met 60 years earlier. Her name was Olive Brassno, and she was a very beautiful midget whom I met about 1940 at the Palace Theater in my hometown of Rockford, Ill. As I watched the movie, memories of our friendship came back to me.

When I was 5 years old, my mother was employed as the theater's cleaning woman, and I usually went to work with Mom on Saturdays. Being at the Palace was like fairy-tale time for me. The theater featured vaudeville acts on the bill as well as movies, and all the performers made over me. I loved them all.

Some of them knew my Uncle Art and Aunt Morna Monette, who had been in vaudeville and the circus. It was fun to hear about their years in show business, many years before I was born.

The theater featured vaudeville acts on the bill as well as movies.

Mom had to be at the theater by 6 a.m. to get everything done before the box office opened at noon.

Cleaning a theater was a lot of work, but I loved being there. First we walked up and down the rows of seats, carrying a bucket and a basket. Trash went into the bucket, and gloves, scarves, shoes, hankies, jewelry, billfolds, purses and many other things were put in the basket.

We turned over the purses and billfolds to the manager, who tried to locate their owners. The other things in the basket went into lost and found, and after 30 days we could have whatever had gone unclaimed.

We could keep any loose money we found on the floor, too. We usually found quite a few coins, and even a bill once in a while. It made working fun—like a treasure hunt—as we wondered what we might find next. No two days cleaning the theater were alike.

While Mom used a carpet sweeper in the aisles, I wiped down each seat and checked for gum. Then Mom mopped the floor under the seats.

Then it was time to check backstage to see what needed doing. Sometimes we cleaned the empty dressing rooms. We always had to clean the room where the orchestra stayed between shows.

It was always a mess, with cigarette butts, bottles and trash. I wiped the tables, and Mom mopped the floor.

After we had tended to the restrooms, we had to clean the manager's office and check the snack area. Finally we did the box office, and then we were done.

When we were finished, Mom and I ate the sack lunches we had brought from home. By that time, many of the performers and the manager had arrived. I usually stayed at the theater while my mom left to meet my dad to do their weekly shopping. Before she left, Mom always gave me 10 cents to buy popcorn and root beer to snack on while I watched the show. The manager was a good friend of my parents and looked out for me.

A movie marquee from the World War II years advertises free admission to the show with the purchase of a war bond. The movie advertised, Destination Tokyo, *places the date in 1943; it starred Cary Grant, John Garfield and Alan Hale. There were still theaters, like the Palace, that featured vaudeville acts in the war years.*

I loved watching rehearsals, which sometimes went on while we were cleaning. Backstage, I watched the women put on their stage makeup and wigs. The costumes were beautiful, all glittery with sequins. Once in a while, someone would put makeup on me and try to show me some simple tap steps. I loved it!

The men in the orchestra made me their pet. They passed a lot of time playing cards, and they tried to teach me how to play. Many of those fellows were family men, lonely for their own children, and I probably reminded them of their families.

The stage show included a variety of acts featuring dancers, dogs and acrobats. Sometimes there were singers and skits. I ran errands for the whole troupe, and I usually got a nickel or a dime for each trip. I would run across the street to the Metropolitan Dime Store to get all kinds of items. And they always asked me if I would like some of what they were eating. I grew to love those performers, and they were very good to me.

The first time I saw Olive Brassno, she was dressed almost like me in a cotton dress, white socks and brown, low-cut shoes. At first I thought she was a little girl. But when I talked to her, I noticed that she talked like a grown-up and wore nail polish. Her voice was a little high pitched, but she was very graceful, even though she wasn't as tall as I was at age 6. When she put on her makeup and costume, I thought she was beautiful. She looked just like a real live doll.

Olive and her partner, George, danced ballroom as well as tap dancing. They were so cute together. George usually spent his spare time playing cards with the orchestra members. He smoked big cigars and treated me like a little girl even though I was taller than he was.

Olive hated to go out on the street. If she was in costume and needed something from the dime store, I always went to get it for her. On Saturday mornings she dressed like me, and we looked like two little girls tripping down the sidewalk. We had so much fun together!

Olive told me that she and George had played in a circus movie a few years earlier. I know now that it was *Charlie Chan at the Circus*. Just last year, I finally got a copy on video, and I have watched it many, many times.

Olive also told me that they were in another movie along with almost all the "little people" from all over the United States. Back then, I didn't realize that she must have meant *The Wizard of Oz*. But try as I might, I've never been able to identify her when I watch my video copy.

All the performers who appeared at the Palace worked a circuit that took them from theater to theater in towns across the country and back again. Whenever they returned to the Palace, we enjoyed a happy reunion. They often brought gifts and pictures for me.

The last time I saw George and Olive, they told me they were going to get off the road and move to California. Olive gave me a precious beaded purse that I cherished for many years.

My mom worked at the Palace for several years. Even after she quit, I would stop by every once in a while, going in through the stage door to see if anyone I knew was playing the bill.

Soon, however, live stage shows became a thing of the past. When they ended, it was truly the end of an era. I missed my old friends. Uncle Art subscribed to *Billboard*, and once in a while, when I was visiting him and Aunt Morna, I would recognize a name in that showbiz journal.

I know beyond a doubt that Olive and George and all of my other old friends from the Palace must be gone by now.

But how nice to know that in the halls of my memory, I can bring them all back and return to those bygone days when we were all together at the Palace! ❖

Pals of the '30s

By Marie Yockim

Six in the morning is pretty early for a 6-year-old girl to be up and all dressed. It was a warm, sunny day in September and an exciting day, as this was the first day of school. My friend, Arline, was going to meet me halfway, and then we would walk to school together.

This was 1931 and the start of many new things for us. For starters, we wore new, black, shiny oxfords and new dresses, and we each had a new fall coat.

On the second day of school the teacher wanted everyone to get up in front of the class and recite a poem, tell a story or do whatever they could do to entertain the class for five minutes. Arline and I, the two songbirds, sang a current hit, *When It's Springtime in the Rockies*. We had heard it on the radio and at the movies.

Movies were very important to us in the Good Old Days. We were movie buffs at that young age—mainly "B" Westerns and musicals.

Arline and I even tried something new at the movies when we were in the eighth grade. A movie was being shown at the Orpheum Theater that we wanted to see, mainly because the ad said "For Adults Only." We thought we could pass for adults if we dressed up. We put on our best dresses and borrowed our mothers' heels, purses, gloves and hats. We also borrowed quite a bit of their makeup. We figured we looked at least 18 or 21.

We walked to the box office and plunked down 15 cents each. Smiling at us, the lady said, "Adult tickets are 25 cents each." We each added 10 cents more and went into the darkened theater. We sat in the back row.

We didn't enjoy the show, as we didn't understand most of it. On the way home, we took off our high heels so we could walk better.

After that episode, we went back to Saturday matinees. We didn't mention the adult movie again, although we noticed a few looks between the ticket lady and the manager sometimes when we went to the matinees. ❖

Friday Night At the Movies

By Beverly Hill McKinney

*D*addy, can we go to the movies tonight?" I asked.

"Yes, as soon as dinner is over and the dishes are done."

"Is it Westerns again? I really get tired of them."

"Oh, I think they're exciting," Dad replied.

Friday night at the movies was a tradition my parents began before I was born. I was raised in the 1940s in the small Northern California town of Pacific Grove. Every Friday night we walked the few blocks to the movie theater. My two older brothers and sister always ran ahead, anxious to get to the theater and see their friends. Since we lived in such a small town, many of our friends and neighbors met at the theater.

Friday was always Western night. Roy Rogers, Gene Autry, the Lone Ranger and Hopalong Cassidy were our favorite heroes. I think I saw almost all the movies those actors ever made.

Our family had a designated seating order at the movies. Mom sat at the end of the row, my brothers and sister next to her, and then Dad, with me at the end. Dad always sat close to me because I was the talkative one and he had to tell me numerous times to be quiet. But most importantly, I shared his popcorn.

Dad's favorite part of the movies was the weekly newsreel. World War II was drawing to a close, and he waited all week to see what was happening in the world. At home we listened to the news on our small radio, but seeing the action on the screen was a special treat.

Mom liked the sing-along that came after the newsreels. A bouncing ball and the words to a song appeared on the screen below a short cartoon. The song went with the story, and we sang as the ball bounced from word to word.

My brothers and sister always waited patiently for the coming attractions. Since they were older, often they were allowed to go to movies again on the weekend. The cartoons were my favorite, and it didn't matter which was showing as long as it was colorful and funny.

One particular Friday night stands out in my memory. I was only about 6 years old. We arrived at the theater and Dad and Mom purchased popcorn for us all. They usually bought one box for Mom to share with my brothers and sister

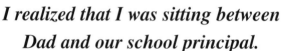

I realized that I was sitting between Dad and our school principal.

and another for Dad to share with me.

We hurried into the theater. After sitting down, I realized that I was sitting between Dad and our grammar school principal. Dad said hello to him as the lights dimmed. Then the movie started, and we were at once engrossed in the newsreel and coming attractions.

As the cartoon began, I started to eat Dad's popcorn, which usually lasted through the entire movie. But the Western that night was especially exciting, and I ate faster than ever.

The movie ended. We were exiting the theater when Dad said, "Bev, you didn't eat much popcorn tonight. Are you OK? Something wrong?"

"What do you mean?" I replied. "I ate your whole box!"

"No, look, I have almost a full box left."

"Oh, no!" I exclaimed.

I suddenly realized what I had done. I looked back toward the theater entrance where my principal stood with a wide smile on his face—and an empty popcorn box in his hand. ❖

Saturdays and Sundaes

By Florine Cherwin

*I*t's a far, far better thing that I do. ..." The mellifluous voice caressed our beating hearts as we tearfully watched him walk with unfaltering steps to the guillotine. Rapt with emotion, our adolescent bodies clung to our seats as we accepted the cruel finale to *A Tale of Two Cities*.

Every Saturday afternoon my bosom friend, Emily, and I slipped into the neighborhood theater for a dime. Children under 12 got in for a nickel. Movies were our Land of Oz. We fantasized with lovely Norma Shearer; romped with the effervescent Clara Bow; and suffered with Bette Davis when she was whipped by fate in *Now Voyager* and *Dark Victory*. We agonized with Janet Gaynor and Charles Farrell during their reunion in *Seventh Heaven*. Ah, sweet romance!

Those were the days when movie stars sent out 9 by 12-inch glossies of themselves on request. Between us, Emily and I accumulated more than 300 pictures. Today they would be collectibles but, alas, they disappeared with our pimples and buckled galoshes—thanks to our mothers' annual, thorough, no-hidey-holes-spared spring cleaning.

After our emotional Saturday movie-viewing safari came the *pièce de résistance*: a stop at the next-door ice-cream parlor for an unforgettable fudge sundae or banana split. This immaculate, cozy store served homemade, butter-yellow ice cream that could turn enemies into friends. White, lacy, starched curtains covered the sparkling windows like costume jewelry and introduced customers to a room equipped with three small, round, wrought iron tables, each fitted with three matching chairs. Four booths along one wall seated four each in close comfort.

Photo courtesy the United States Department of Agriculture

Hot-fudge sundaes were our favorite. Two scoops—way beyond regulation size—of ice cream were pressed into a tulip-shaped glass. A huge dollop of fudge on top spread out and moved slowly down the sides before it merged with the whipped cream (*real* whipped cream whipped in a hand-operated creamer). A generous sprinkling of whole and chopped pecans was added before a bold, red cherry completed the picture of our "most wanted."

Our second choice was the banana split—for only a quarter! Three scoops of ice cream hid a large banana cut in half lengthwise. Strawberry, pineapple and butterscotch-flavored syrups covered the scoops. Marshmallow, chocolate and caramel flavors were also available. Chopped nuts, whipped cream and a cherry atop each scoop made this a triple treat. We especially loved the whipped cream, tossed on top with reckless abandon.

On our way out we had to pass the candy counter. Of course we stopped to look and point. And when our hesitation became quite apparent, the proprietress, a plump, grandmotherly woman wearing a crisp, white uniform, offered to sell us her largest chocolate nougat bar, cut in half and put into two separate bags—for 2 cents.

All of this gorging would provoke an avalanche of no-nos today. But Emily and I remained thin and trim, perhaps because our most available transportation was on foot. We walked miles to and from school every day. "Couch potato" wasn't in our vocabulary.

To us, our Saturdays together spawned a precious camaraderie filled with girl talk, boy talk, giggles and an exchange of opinions, ideas, hopes and dreams. Now these Saturdays have become a conversation piece—the day filled with the sweetest memories of growing up. ❖

The Mayfair

By Arlene Storch Rizzo

Although the little town of Hillside, N.J., where I grew up, encompassed only two square miles, it boasted a popular movie theater called The Mayfair. The theater sat at our town boundary line—really, it was closer to Newark—but the distance didn't stop us from frequenting it. We spent the Saturday afternoons of our childhood at the Mayfair's matinee. Admission was only 25 cents during the late 1940s, and that was for two full-length feature films plus four cartoons. It didn't matter when you went in or how long you stayed. You could watch the films over and over if you wished.

Sometimes my girlfriends and I took the No. 10 bus from Liberty Avenue; it dropped us off right in front of the Mayfair. We usually walked to save the bus fare so we had extra money for a candy bar, bonbons or a bakery treat on the way home.

We waited breathlessly for the boys to slip their arms around our shoulders.

I always made sure to save 3 cents from what Mother had given me because I passed Goldstein's Bakery, and Mrs. Goldstein always gave us a cinnamon bun or cheese bun for 3 cents late on Saturday afternoon. My girlfriend, Mary Jane, and I lived the farthest from the theater, but we had that extra treat to look forward to on the way home.

We knew of a shortcut past the railway. Before we reached the movie house, there was a huge field with a high hill to climb. On the way home, though, we would all lie down on our sides and, with a gentle push from one of our friends, we could roll all the way down the hill.

As we approached our teens, our "movie day" became Friday night. All the Hillside High School crowd went. We went with our boyfriends. Sitting there in the dark movie house, we waited breathlessly for the boys we were with to slip their arms around our shoulders and draw us close, where we remained until intermission.

Intermission was the signal for all of us girls to visit the Mayfair's red velvet powder room. There we would meet the girlfriend we hadn't seen since Friday afternoon classes and trade secrets and giggle about who was with whom.

"Did you see who Sonny was with tonight?"

By now we had graduated from 3-cent bakery treats to frequent Uncle Tom's Pizza Tavern after a movie. A whole pizza cost $1–$1.25. Either our boyfriends paid, or five or six of us chipped in a quarter apiece.

After I began going steady (which, back then, meant dating someone exclusively and letting the whole world know it by wearing his high-school ring on a gold chain around my neck), I began to collect the free dishes that were offered at the Mayfair. The price of admission included a free dish or cup each week until you completed a whole set of dishes. My first set was pink with cascading gray pussy willows.

Sometimes, just as Robert Taylor was about to embrace Barbara Stanwyck for the long-awaited kiss, someone's dish would crash onto the cement floor. This always brought rousing applause from the audience, and that long-awaited kiss was lost forever. But that didn't happen too often.

The dishes we used at home had been collected by Mother and Grandma, both of whom were avid movie fans, along with Aunt Alice and Aunt Dotty. Mother's regular movie night was Thursday. I could hardly wait for her to come home and give me a preview of what I would see the next evening.

There is a saying that "art imitates life," and that was certainly true of movies in the late 1940s and early 1950s. Life was simpler, nostalgic, free of violence and oh, so happy and carefree!

Our heroes of the silver screen were played by such movie greats as Clark Gable, Henry Fonda and Cary Grant. They were teamed romantically with beautiful Lana Turner, Elizabeth Taylor, Maureen O'Hara and, my favorite, Doris Day. I watched and studied her every move, and I thought her gorgeous clothes were breathtaking.

And so, once a week, we escaped our rather ordinary lives and fantasized about the beautiful places, adventures and romance that we were sure lay just ahead for all of us—thanks to Hollywood and our wonderful little Mayfair movie theater. ❖

A Dime's Worth

By Agnes Moench

When I was growing up in West Texas during the 1940s, Saturday afternoon movies were a big treat for my friend Loretta and me. Occasionally, the Mecca Theater carried a double feature, and then we *really* got our dime's worth of entertainment.

These features at the matinees were almost always Western films. Among our favorite cowboy stars were Randolph Scott (by far my favorite), William Boyd as Hopalong Cassidy, and Allan "Rocky" Lane or Wild Bill Elliott as Red Ryder. John Mack Brown, Gene Autry and, later, Rex Allen were also popular names in many early Western movies.

To my knowledge, none of these films ever received an Academy Award, and I doubt the stars were nominated for Best Actor recognition. But in our young minds, these actors were the best. They were our heroes.

The plot was usually the same—only the actors were different. Each week we watched the leading man and his sidekick bring law and order to the Old West by putting cattle rustlers behind bars, foiling stagecoach or bank holdups, or saving a pretty girl from being swindled out of her gold mine by a bunch of tough guys. But before justice could be served, the scoundrels had to be captured. When one of the heroes got word of some misdeed, he would jump (sometimes from a second-story window) onto the back of his faithful horse and gallop across the silver screen in hot pursuit of the culprits.

Of course, every young heart in the theater beat a little faster as our hero went up against gunfire and a messy fistfight following a long, hard chase. But we knew that Hoppy, Scott or Red Ryder would bring back his man. In some cases, they captured the whole gang of ruffians.

There is no getting around it; we did see violence and corruption on Saturday afternoons. It's also a fact that the movies ended with *good* overcoming *bad*. I believe that is why none of us wanted to be the bad guy when we played "cowboys" or acted out one of the movies. ❖

Tarzan and Other Heroes

By Lorraine A. Warren

Aaaayyaa! This yell heard more than a half-century ago still echoes in my mind. Perhaps it does in yours also if, as a youngster, you attended the Saturday afternoon matinee at the local movie theater as I did from 1942–1945.

If Johnny Weissmuller were living today, I would probably still expect to see him swinging from tree to tree through the jungle as he did in his portrayal of the legendary Tarzan. I can remember imitating Tarzan in our jungle, where a rope hung from a huge pepper tree in our back yard in Southern California.

Tarzan was only one of the heroes we went to see at the Saturday matinee.

My two cousins and I would receive our long-awaited quarter each Saturday. No accountant could have been more astute in utilizing those 25 cents. We knew bus fare to North Hollywood was a nickel each way. Admission to the Valley Theatre was a dime. (We didn't attend the matinee at the El Portal. It was too expensive at 16 cents.)

Treats, such as a bag of popcorn, a soft drink or a candy bar, were a nickel each. This caused a financial crisis if we wanted to have two treats, one purchased before curtain time and one during intermission. My cousin Billy, being a boy, simply hitchhiked home, using his bus fare for the extra treat. Being girls, my cousin Berta and I were not allowed to hitchhike, and it was understood we'd come home on the bus.

If we had been lucky enough to scavenge enough returnable bottles during the week, we could have our extra treat *and* ride the bus both

Johnny Weissmuller played Tarzan
in movies from 1932–1948.

ways. The going rate for returnable bottles was a penny each. As an alternative, we could walk the three miles into town to the theater, and we did that more than once.

Berta maintains that she would have walked much farther to see Gene Autry. She "fell in love" for the first time at age 8 when she saw Autry on the screen. If the truth were told, she might still be in love with him!

We had to be the first to arrive to get the prized front-row aisle seats.

Along with our friends, we cheered when our heroes Hopalong Cassidy, Roy Rogers, Buster Crabbe and Randolph Scott got there in the nick of time. I can still hear the cavalry's arrival just at that last moment, always heralded by the sound of the bugle.

But not all Saturday matinees featured cowboys. And even though I was prone to motion sickness as a child, I am sure I would not have hesitated to sail away with those great swashbucklers Douglas Fairbanks Jr. and Errol Flynn.

There were horror movies, too. I don't remember which actor frightened me most—Boris Karloff as Frankenstein, or Lon Chaney Jr. as the Wolfman. The background music alone gave me goose bumps, and I ate my popcorn faster and faster as the tension mounted.

We watched the newsreels impatiently because they always preceded the featured cartoon and the double feature.

Two movies, a cartoon, a serial and a newsreel—all for a dime! Those theaters no longer exist, but I'll be happy to go back there any Saturday afternoon in my memories. Be sure to bring a nickel for the bus ride home! ❖

Projecting a Good Image

By Charles Herring

*I*t only paid $11 a week. Still, it was a dream job for a high-school boy. In 1945, at age 15, I landed the job of projectionist for our town's only movie theater—The Olive. Wow! It was my first job away from Daddy's store. As a result, it instilled in me invaluable lessons in work ethics, self-sufficiency and lasting memories.

And those lessons—they began early. In fact, the first time I functioned as "the picture-show operator," I got into trouble.

My job officially began with the Monday afternoon matinee. Everybody in town knew that starting time for the Monday, Wednesday and Friday matinees was 3:30 p.m. That first day I could hardly wait to start. And that was the problem: I didn't—wait to start, that is.

Being a movie projectionist was a dream job for a high school boy.

Watching the seconds tick off a clock in the projection room, and being extremely nervous, at precisely 3:30 p.m., I started the show.

The homemade communication system between the second-floor projection room and the ticket office below was about as simple as it could be. A 2-inch pipe had been installed vertically through the walls to connect the two areas. Elbows on each end of the pipe served as mouthpieces.

To alert the person on the other end to whom you wanted to talk, you blew into the mouthpiece to make a tuba-like sound. Within seconds of my starting the show that first day, a blast came on the pipe. It was the ticket saleslady—an adult.

"Yes?"

"What do you mean, starting already?" the voice on the pipe asked angrily. "I still have a line of people down here buying tickets. Young man! *I* tell you when to start. Don't you *ever* start again without me telling you to!"

I never did again.

My job as The Olive's projectionist settled into a routine after that. The responsibility it required of me surely benefited me later in life. A typical week went like this:

On Sunday afternoon I would lug the heavy metal, octagonal reel cans that had been delivered to the theater's entrance up the steps to the projection room. I then spent several hours preparing for the week ahead.

I had to splice preview sections, show-time day headings and commercials together in proper sequence.

Then I had to unpack and identify the reels of film for the upcoming Monday matinee, and assure that they were unbroken and rewound.

Then I cleaned and serviced the projection equipment, especially the housings and mirrors containing the powerful carbon arc lights.

Finally, I threaded the reels of film into the two 35-millimeter Simplex E projectors.

Occasionally the film would break while a movie was in progress. The speed with which I could thread a reel of film into those projectors became a source of pride for me. Even the briefest interruption brought hollers and whistles from the audience, not to mention a toot on the pipe from the boss. Humbly I say: I was fast.

Most of the preparatory tasks were repeated as the week progressed. Then came Saturday. That was "the big day," not only for me, but for all The Olive's employees.

A serial followed by a Western movie was kicked off at noon on Saturdays. I ran them over and over until nearly 10 p.m. Then we paused and "took up" tickets for a different movie. Its showing became known as "the midnight show." Regardless of the advertised feature, I don't remember the theater ever having an empty seat for that show.

An important rule applied to the midnight show: It had to end before midnight. Blue laws back then prohibited movies from being shown on Sundays. Those laws were rigidly enforced. Fortunately, "The End" always flashed on the screen just before midnight.

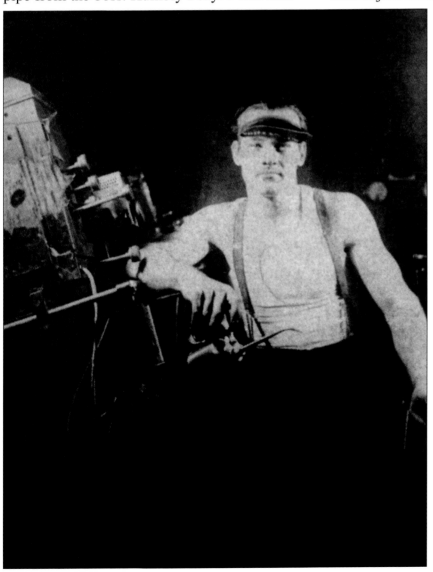

Detailed memories of that first job away from Daddy's store remain vivid for me. I can still close my eyes and see the intricate details of those projectors, smell the burning carbon arcs, hear the intermittent sound that film makes when being jerked along by sprockets … "Uh oh, that take-up wheel is rubbing the housing. I'll have to straighten it when it gets empty again."

Perhaps such vivid memories are why I still enjoy the old, classic movies on cable TV so much. When I see some old movies being played again, quite often I will nudge my wife and say, "I remember showing that one. Hey, look! There was the changeover dot. Did you see it?" and my mind drifts back to another time, another place. ❖

No, the photograph at left isn't of the author, but it does give a look at the projection room of the Band Box Theatre, Springfield, Ohio, in 1934. The projectionist, Phil Rosskopf, was probably a lot more composed than the author on his first job away from his father's store.

Free Shows And Popcorn

By Sylvia Oberle

ow I loved that popcorn machine! The shining, fire-engine-red vehicle with its yellow-spoked wheels was the apple of my eye. I watched every detail when the popcorn man scooped and poured the kernels into the silver kettle. In a few minutes, those kernels would lift the lid with frantic, dancing, jumping pops and spill over into the flat bottom until half the window was filled with a snowdrift of white popcorn.

Near the front of the machine, a little iron man whirled 'round, his arms turning a small drum of roasted peanuts. I never tired of watching the little gnome, but I knew I had to make way for other customers.

"Me one too, Daddy!" I called in my eager 5-year-old voice.

My popcorn would be free because the popcorn man was my own father.

"Me one too, Daddy!" A baritone voice in strained falsetto sounded just behind me. Everyone laughed while customers jostled and pushed toward the bright red popcorn machine. The young man paid cheerfully though he was laughing all the while with the popcorn man about his joke. With a smile, the popcorn man poured rich, coconut-oil "butter" over the large, white kernels and handed a carton to me. *My* Jolly Time popcorn box would be free of charge because the popcorn man was my own father.

On this particular Saturday night in July 1938, my brothers ran over to help finish my box of Jolly Time. The boys played tag in the parking lot nearby, and I tagged along. I ran away from the mud around the parked cars because Mother had dressed me in a blue taffeta slip covered with a dress of handmade lace. It was tied with a blue ribbon sash.

Soon I was running around the parking lot with no brothers or friends in sight. I ran out into the blocked-off street. Looking up, I could see I had wandered to the other side.

This short street in our small village of Boyd, Wis., was ideal for an outdoor movie theater because it was on a natural hill. In the 1940s, free shows entertained friends and neighbors in rural Wisconsin during the summer season. Merchants in the small towns sponsored the events on Friday or Saturday nights to entice more shopping and community spirit.

"What's a movie without popcorn?" Father had said to my mother when he purchased the popcorn machine. She went along with his venture quite reluctantly.

Facing page: *The Popcorn Man* by Jay Killian, House of White Birches nostalgia archives

Popping corn at free shows somehow reminded her of a carnival, and she couldn't quite approve of *them*. She did, however, like the idea of getting the family shopping done on Saturday night while the kids watched the show.

On this particular Saturday night, I felt lost and more than a little worried. I was just a bit turned around, but that was spooky to a 5-year-old in the dark. I looked up at the movie screen, a huge cotton sheet (something heavier if your town could afford it), stretched high on the side of the feed mill. I could see the final feature of the show was almost over because the cowboys in the white hats were about to catch the cowboys in the black hats.

The movie features were always shown in the same order: *Movietone News*; a comedy, like *Felix the Cat*; and the main feature, starring actors like Gene Autry, Gary Cooper and Randolph Scott. Since it was near the end of the last feature, I knew that I must find Dad and the popcorn wagon soon.

The author's treasure: the little iron gnome with the drum of roasted peanuts.

In the dark, I walked across and in front of friends and neighbors sitting on blankets on the hill. Some sat on planks placed across barrels. A few others sat in their own folding lawn chairs.

I just couldn't see anyone I knew. Panicked that I might miss my ride home, I ran over to the sidewalk in front of a busy tavern. I quivered when a 6-foot man and another, almost as tall, stood there, using rough language and smoking.

My feet fairly flew away from the tavern and past the local garage. I saw a man under a car. The thought crossed my mind that maybe he was dead—all I could see were legs sticking out. I didn't need thoughts like *those* to add to my fright!

Running faster till I was quite out of breath, I reached the grocery store. I hoped I might find my mother inside, just finishing her grocery shopping. I felt safer inside the store since my grandfather often gave me pennies to spend there. Sometimes I'd buy Kit Kat caramels that

came five in a pack for 2 cents. If I had a whole nickel, I could buy a Hershey chocolate bar.

I ran past the candy counter and down the aisle with the bulk cookie cabinets that contained my favorite windmill cookies and the ones with the thick, white frosting. I looked up and down the aisles, but Mother wasn't there. She wasn't in the bread aisle buying the 29-cent Buries Bread. Those shelves were nearly empty now that free show night was almost over.

In the cooler, I saw quarts of milk in glass bottles with thick paper caps, and fresh meat waiting to be cut. I trotted past the Plowboy and Velvet tobacco and back to the candy counter. I had no pennies to spend on this Saturday night. And worst of all, no mother, no brothers in the whole of Leubstorf's Grocery Store!

Back out on the sidewalk, I zigged and zagged around small groups of adults who were still visiting. My heart began beating faster, and I could feel a lump in my throat. Then I glimpsed the action of the little clown as he twirled 'round and 'round. I was thrilled to see that little iron man because I knew he was connected to Dad's popcorn wagon. That red wagon with its yellow lights was a sight for sore eyes!

Soon I saw my tall, handsome father, his white dress shirt rolled at the sleeves, scooping up the last cartons of Jolly Time popcorn. He was cleaning out the "old maids" in preparation for our next free-show trip.

Ah! Safety awaited me with Dad and our popcorn wagon. Dad smiled down at me as I skipped joyfully into his arms. He boosted me up, and I took the rest of the peanuts from the clown's little drum. My fright over being lost disappeared like vapor.

Many years later, our popcorn wagon was sold to an antique dealer. But I kept a treasure: the little iron man that I could see that night turning 'round and 'round, roasting peanuts in his little drum. ❖

Off to the Movies!

By Angie Monnens

On that special Saturday, bath time began earlier than usual. We girls, dressed in our gingham dresses, and the boys, in starched white shirts, had looked forward to this treat for weeks. Each of us had a dime knotted in the corner of a hankie so we wouldn't lose it. Finally we were all ready and happily raced uptown.

The presentation, a double feature with Charlie Chaplin and the Three Stooges, would last into the afternoon. As we neared the opera house, a huge cream-colored brick building in desperate need of a new coat of paint, kids and adults were already gathered outside.

This building directly behind the depot was used as an auditorium for a variety of entertainments. It was larger than our 10-room house, with a ceiling so high that we could barely see the chandeliers!

On movie day, the hall filled to capacity in a hurry. Those who came late had to stand along the walls. Small scuffles ensued when someone tried to cut in line, but the old constable kept order without any serious confrontations.

Seating so many people as the crowd grew, we could hear the clanging of folding chairs echo through the building. Now we waited patiently for the movie to start and began to eat the popcorn Mama had sent along in a brown paper sack. We ate slowly, hoping it would last through the movies. It didn't take long before the butter leaked through the bag, and what better place to wipe our greasy hands than on our dresses? Of course, Mama was unhappy when she saw grease spots on our Sunday clothes.

But now the time had come! We heard the trumpets—"Ta-ta-ta!"—as the title flashed on the makeshift screen and the show began!

For two and a half hours, we laughed at the antics of the stars who got into situations that kept us on the edge of our seats. We watched as the Three Stooges poked and slapped each other, and wondered why it didn't seem to hurt.

All the way home we followed suit, trying to make each other laugh. Yet sometimes when one of us poked the other in the eye, or slapped another's face, we found that it wasn't as much fun as the Three Stooges! We promised that no one would tattle and tell Mama what we had tried on the way home. We knew she would scold us, as we had always been taught to treat each other with love. Come to think of it, she probably would have considered the Three Stooges' antics violent!

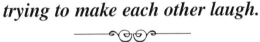

All the way home we followed suit, trying to make each other laugh.

As years passed and movies where shown at our first theater, I became a movie buff. I saw every show, even though it cost a dime. Later, when I was a teenager, it was 35 cents.

The movie bug that bit me as a child stayed with me. After I had graduated, I got a job as a ticket seller at the theater. During the day I worked at Dad's grocery store across the street. Then, in the evenings, I sold movie tickets. After I had the second movie crowd ready for the second show, I could stay and watch for free.

I loved this arrangement. I saw all the best movies ever made in the '30s and '40s—the spectacular follies featuring the dancing of Ginger Rogers, Fred Astaire, Cyd Charisse and Gene Kelly; and the great dramas with the likes of Robert Taylor, Greta Garbo, Tyrone Powers and Gene Tierney.

Movies were so pleasurable then. When we left the theater, we went home floating on a cloud, glad to be alive. What a difference from our reactions to many of today's movies!

If modern life gets you down, put on a movie featuring the Three Stooges or Charlie Chaplin—and laugh till your sides ache. You'll feel great! ❖

Stars Under the Stars

By Robert L. Tefertillar

hose few that are still standing are mostly forlorn and ghost-ridden. They crumble away under summer sun and winter wind, awaiting their demise by a bulldozer to make way for some parking lot, shopping mall or housing development. Those now-lifeless locations have only skeleton remains of speaker posts, marquees and what once was a lively refreshment stand.

Only a few decades ago, the drive-in theater was a place of music and laughter, featuring movieland's most entertaining stars. These sites now await the same undeserved fate as the ornate downtown movie palaces of the past.

My most pleasurable and exciting memories are those of the excursions to the drive-in theater of yesteryear. Hollywood, even in its infancy, made movies to scare the yell out of an audience. The joining of scary films and outdoor drive-in theaters was a marriage made in entertainment heaven for "going steady," puppy-dog-love teenagers.

What a thrill to double- or even triple-date and enjoy a spooky show under a ghostly full moon on a crisp fall evening.

It doesn't take much imagination to picture that the excitement inside the crowded automobile was at least as tense and suspenseful as that on the screen. Fortunately, the "B" movies of the '50s and '60s were the most typical drive-in theater fare, especially the sci-fi and horror flicks.

> *Only a few decades ago, the drive-in was a place of music and laughter.*

The drive-in theaters took a lot of prime real estate, which is what eventually led to their passing. They were located mostly on the outskirts of the city, and the space required was considerable. There had to be room for a gigantic parking lot, gargantuan screen, and a spider web of connecting roads to get in and out without causing a jumbo nightmare of traffic congestion.

Of course, there would also be a large refreshment stand and sizable restroom accommodations. Some of the larger drive-in theaters also featured a kiddie playground complete with teeter-totters, swings, merry-go-round, Ferris wheel and picnic facilities.

Drive-in theaters truly offered something for everybody, every age group and every member of the family. Dad could load up the car with Grandma, Grandpa, Mom, the kids and the neighbor's kids as well for an entire evening's outing. The younger children had their playground and cartoons, the teens their sci-fi and Andy Hardy movies, and the adults their love stories, Westerns and musicals.

Admission to such a cornucopia of entertainment often cost less than a buck for adults and a dime for kids, with the younger children free.

Facing page: *Drive-In Movies* by George Hughes © 1961 SEPS: Licensed by Curtis Publishing

On special nights it was sometimes just $1.25 for a carload of bodies.

That was when the neighbor with the station wagon became a best buddy, although it was truly amazing the amount of humanity that teenagers could cram into one old tin lizzy Ford coupe with a rumble seat.

Then there were the dusk-to-dawn movie marathons, when the screen action started before dark and didn't wind up until daylight. That was when adventurous teenagers with flashlights could truly become an endangered species. This was especially true if they picked a car with a batch of football players

☞ Please do not reveal the middle of this picture! *Jerry's a mousey chemistry prof who invents the greatest drink since Dracula discovered bloody marys.*

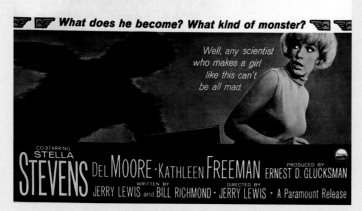

Jerry Lewis was one of the most popular comedic actors—both in drive-ins and in theaters—in the 1950s and 1960s. He teamed up with Dean Martin for many comedies, and in 1952 the duo was named the most popular actors in America by the Quigley Poll of moviegoers. The Nutty Professor was released in 1963.

and their dates to highlight with their hand-held spotlights.

Talk about "lights, camera, action"—movie patrons got all three!

The drive-in theater was heaven-sent entertainment for pubescent youngsters who had "wheels" in the form of bicycles. Right after supper, they and their buddies could leave for the movies. They could enjoy the films without having to sneak in an unlocked side door, as was often the case during the Saturday-afternoon cowboy double features, thus preserving the dime admission for candy or a comic book.

The highest points outside the drive-in theater were always the choice seats, just as the balcony or front-row seats were the best vantage points in the indoor theaters. The only difficulty was hearing the sound over the traffic on the nearby highway.

But the free admission compensated, although one could not dump pop or popcorn on the kids below, like in the theater balcony. Still, there was always some excitement, especially when the movies ended and the cars drove away with the speakers still inside the window.

Quite often there was a fender bender or two when the exit spaces became jammed, so the evening usually was satisfactory for the bike brigade, of which I was a member.

Today's movie enthusiast has more movies to view than ever before, thanks to VHS tapes, DVDs, cable and satellite. However, there were no more-entertaining movies than those shown outdoors on that giant screen and viewed through the windshield of an automobile. It was sometimes hard to see, often hard to hear, and mosquito repellent was a necessity. A sudden, unexpected rainstorm could be a disaster. But it still was a novel and entertaining way to see a show.

There are still a few drive-in theaters in operation, but they are few and far between. The drive-in theater, like those wonderful old movie fan magazines, will soon be only pleasurable nostalgic memories of yesterday. ❖

The High Cost of Entertainment

By Bill Crocker

I recently returned to Fredonia, N.Y., to visit friends and my old stomping grounds. I spent most of the early mornings at The Hook and Ladder Deli, sampling the wonderful pecan buns and good coffee and renewing old friendships. Eliot, Wally and Jim were usually there, and our conversations revolved around our childhood memories of Fredonia. One of these memories was the Winter Garden Theater.

"Remember the Saturday matinees?" Wally recalled one morning.

"Yeah, geez, remember what we paid? Twenty-five cents!" responded Eliot in his usual high-spirited manner. That got us started.

At the site of the old Winter Garden Theater, the top portion of the fire escape and the theater balcony door can be seen in the upper left corner.

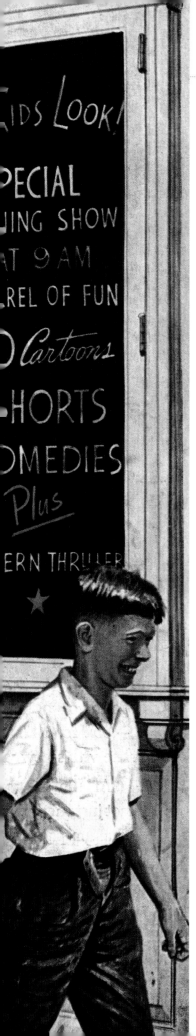

Today, the 1891 Fredonia Opera House stands as a beautiful example of Victorian architecture. Its renovation is a wonderful testimony to Fredonia's interest in maintaining a tie with the town's very historic past.

However, in 1948, it was an entertainment center of a different sort. Then it was called the Winter Garden Theater, and it was the only movie house in town.

It was where we spent our Saturday afternoons as kids. It was where we as teenagers curled up in a darkened balcony corner with our best girl. It was also where the balcony rocked when several kids did an old version of the "wave." As it turned out, there was a reason for the movement. During the 1994 renovation, workers discovered that the balcony had never been anchored properly.

In 1948, the price of admission was 10 cents. For another 10 cents, you could get a bag of popcorn and a Coke. And if you were able to wheedle an additional 5 cents from parents who were looking forward to a kid-free afternoon, you could get a candy bar. So for 25 cents, you got plenty of good stuff to eat, two features, one serial and one or two cartoons—heaven, to be sure!

"But, do you remember when the admission price shot up to 12 cents?" Jim said. "We knew that we couldn't afford that."

Whoever was responsible for devising the plan to obtain the extra 2 cents should have been knighted. It was worthy of a Nobel Prize for creative thinking. A metal fire escape extended to the Temple Street sidewalk from the theater balcony door on the second floor. We decided that we could each get the 2 cents from the kids who couldn't afford the 12 cents. In exchange, we would open the fire escape door from the balcony and let those kids enter the theater. They paid 2 cents for the afternoon and we got the extra money we wanted.

But there was some danger for these 2-cent kids. Not everyone wanted to chance it because the street-level entrance to the fire escape was just a few feet from the police station's front door, and in full view of street traffic. It was a little too exciting for the faint of heart, halfway up the fire escape, to hear Chief Thompson yell, "Hey you kids! Get off that fire escape! I want to see you in the station, *now*!"

However, there were enough kids with a couple of pennies to spend and the guts to challenge authority to allow us to continue our criminal activities for some time.

This memory of my childhood, like many others, is significantly enhanced when shared with old friends. It is part of growing up in a place where my roots run five generations deep and more than 150 years into the past. It is a memory of a place where most people are quite content to remain all of their lives. These people unwittingly provide a pleasant homecoming for those of us who left town and, in some ways, wish we hadn't. ❖

To Be Continued …

By Dorothy Coleman

I hear Dad stropping his razor on the leather strap that hangs by the mirror on the wall in the summer kitchen. I hurry to join him. Watching Dad shave is one of my favorite things. He covers his face with a layer of foamy lather using a stubby shaving brush that he stirs briskly in a mug to create more lather.

Then he starts the scary part. Pulling that very sharp razor blade down his cheek, he leaves a gaping hole in the white lather. He does it again and more lather disappears. He continues until all the white foam has vanished. Next, he picks up the bottle of Bay Rum, sprinkles some on both hands, and splashes it on his strong, handsome face.

"Now, I'm ready for a kiss from my little girl!" I throw my arms around his neck as he lifts me and swings me around in the air.

This is a Saturday ritual. We go to the movies on Saturday night. Dad comes home early. Mother makes an early supper. I give up roller skating, tree climbing and rope jumping.

In the early 1920s, we are lucky to have a movie theater in our little town of Fawn Grove, Pa., that shows silent movies. The theater is on the second floor above the sewing factory. For us, it is just a few steps past the next-door neighbor and we are there. Everyone in town turns out for the weekly entertainment.

There is a large stage in the front about three feet above the main floor. The curtain covering the stage is canvas with a country scene painted in the center and ads around the sides. On movie night, the curtain rolls up to display a white screen on which we will see an action-packed drama unfold to enthrall us.

The balcony has a few rows of seats with the projection room in the middle. Seats below the balcony flank the stairs of the entrance and are raised above the main floor. Mother and Dad choose seats there. Other youngsters like me always sit in the front seats! My brother sits with his friends. Admission is 15 cents for adults and 10 cents for children.

Oh, the movies! How well I remember *The Perils of Pauline* with Pearl White. Mary Pickford was a sweet young thing to be adored. The Gish sisters, Dorothy and Lillian, played in many of those silent films. We laugh uproariously at the antics of Charlie Chaplin.

When the lights go out, we quiet down for an exciting evening. We hear the whirr as the metal reel unwinds to reveal the magical scenes. Lights flash on and off the white screen. Now the picture show begins.

During the absorbing feature presentation, there might be a tear in the film that halts the show. The lights come on. Necks crane in the direction of the projection room. We hear the whirring of the reel as they fix the problem. There are a few flashes on the screen before the lights go out, and we are once again immersed in the happenings unfolding before our eyes.

After the feature film, the continuation of last week's serial appears. We have waited a week to see if the heroine who was tied to the railroad tracks will be saved by the handsome young hero before the train reaches her. She is! They embrace, and we expect a happy ending.

But not so! The treacherous villain has other ideas. Emerging from behind a boulder, he frightens the heroine's horse. The horse throws her into a raging river—just above the falls! The screen goes blank, and then we see those agonizing words: "To be continued next week"!

I learn about frustration, anticipation, concern, sympathy, anger, despair, excitement, elation, apprehension—a broad spectrum of emotions—from that weekly entertainment in the silent movies of the 1920s. To this day I hate those words "To be continued …"! ❖

Town Days

Chapter Two

Grandma Stamps was the first one gnashing at the bit when it came to town days. Grandma didn't drive, and the weekend was just about the only time she had the chance to get away from the farm. She sure didn't want to waste a minute of the day.

After all, downtown was where the "action" was—however little that might be in small towns and villages. Downtown was where the hub-bub of commerce met the relaxed pleasure of friends and neighbors passing the time of day on a busy sidewalk.

We had a mid-'30s Chevy coupe in my adolescent days, and almost every Saturday morning Mama, Grandma, Uncle Bob, my brother, sister and I crowded into that one-seater for what was then a long 10-mile trip to town. We had three adults and my big brother squeezed across the bench seat, with baby sister in alternating laps. I stretched across the small platform, which filled the space from the top of the seat to the tiny back window of the coupe.

The hustle and bustle of downtown on a Saturday morning was raucous music to the ears of a country boy used mainly to the bawling of cattle or the song of the cicada during the summer. Grandma always wanted to make it to the mid-morning auction down by the feed store, where the auctioneer's chant and the bidders' shouts hypnotized me.

After the auction we walked uptown, where the din of shoppers making their way from shop to shop was only surpassed by the rattle,

> *Whittling and yarn spinning have remained with me through the years, but as for tobacco chewing …*

roar and raucous horns of jalopies skirmishing at the intersections.

We walked Main Street to the "five and dime" store (and a nickel or a dime could actually buy something), or down Commercial Street to the Branson Mercantile where Mama always liked to shop.

Sometimes Mama left my brother and me with the old-timers seated at benches near the barbershop. There I learned the manly arts of whittling, spinning yarns and chewing tobacco. Whittling and yarn spinning have remained with me through all these years, but tobacco chewing lasted only until I mistakenly swallowed some tobacco juice. That was the shortest, most productive anti-tobacco campaign ever devised.

It was well past noon (my stomach told me more like 1:30 p.m.) when Mama and Grandma emerged from their shopping forays. Lunch was the Blue Plate special at the only diner in town, where I also sampled my first soft drink (at least the first one I can remember).

Town days were glitz and glamour and lights after dark. From the pool hall and bar on the wrong side of the tracks to the drugstore with its ubiquitous soda fountain, downtown was everything this country boy could imagine.

By the end of the day, even Grandma was more than happy to head back to the farm. It would be but a short week, after all, until we were crowding into the old Chevy again and headed for another Town Day.

—*Ken Tate*

On the Town

By Dale Simmons

For most people, childhood is a distant realm, a foreign territory long forgotten. For me, it's as close as the next heartbeat. I consider the recollection of childhood memories to be an indulgence. I keep them tucked away in a special place and only bring them forth to be relived when time and circumstances are conducive to proper daydreaming. Now is such a time.

My childhood coincided with the 1940s, and I grew up on a farm near the northern outskirts of Balcarres, Saskatchewan. I attended school there, hiking the distance back and forth every day. Regular chores and homework left me with little time to spend in town during the week, but Saturdays were a different matter. That was when the whole family got to go to town, and it was an adventure to be anticipated all week long.

Living on a working farm meant getting a good start every morning. But come Saturday, we were all up even earlier. Nobody wanted to be late leaving for town. Chores were done in jig time, and after breakfast, everyone rushed to clean up and get changed.

In 1942 that made me one of the richest kids in town come Saturday.

Dad would back the '42 Dodge out of the garage, and just before we piled in for the drive to Balcarres, he'd distribute allowances to us kids. My older sisters did more work and naturally received more money. But I didn't quibble. I got $2 a week for doing my chores, and in 1942 that made me one of the richest kids in town come Saturday.

As soon as we hit Main Street, Dad began scouting for a parking spot. The prime location was in front of the Star Café, but you had to get there early to stake a claim. Oftentimes we were too late and had to settle for second best—just down the block, in front of Crosby's General Store. Once parked, we lost no time abandoning the vehicle and setting off to sample town life. The car was never locked. In those days, privacy and property of others was deemed worthy of respect.

Every weekend, Dad and I got haircuts from Scotty McLeod. Mr. McLeod owned the barbershop and pool hall, and back then, his establishment was an all-male domain. It wasn't that women were officially barred; it was just that ladies had no reason to intrude. And since the need didn't exist, they didn't press the issue. Things have certainly changed.

Dad's haircut always came first, and while waiting my turn, I'd watch in rapt fascination the early morning snooker games. Little boys became distractions if they got too close to the tables, though, so I was restricted to the oak benches that lined the walls. I didn't mind. By standing on

Facing page: *Soda Fountain* by John Slobodnik, House of White Birches nostalgia archives

those benches, I got the best view in the house. Even now, if I close my eyes and concentrate, I can hear the whispered stroke of the cue and the muted *click!* of the balls making contact.

After our haircuts, Dad and I would part company. More often than not he stayed at the barbershop. But I had other places to go and other people to see.

Upon leaving Scotty's, I'd head directly for Salter's Drugstore. There was to be found the best selection of candy in all Balcarres. A glass counter stretched 8 feet long, from Mr. Salter's patent medicine shelves to his magazine display. And what wonders that counter did hold!

Jawbreakers, jellybeans, gumdrops and a dozen other kinds of bulk candy filled trays inside. And in huge jars along the top were peppermint sticks, black licorice pipes, red licorice whips, assorted suckers and great, syrupy chunks of horehound candy.

No matter how often Mr. Salter wiped that counter, it was never free of smudged fingerprints put there by zealous epicures anxious to indicate their preferences. I can still recall the sound of the doors opening on the candy case. They slid along on roller bearings, and when Mr. Salter slid them back, the muted *click-click-click* was music to my ears, not unlike what Ali Baba must have heard when he uttered the words "Open, sesame!"

I sometimes spent an hour selecting my initial 25 cents' worth of candy. Agonizing over the choices was almost as much fun as the consumption itself. And that two bits' worth filled a good-sized paper sack, which, with judicious rationing, kept me munching all day.

I visited other business places as well, but unlike Salter's, my reasons for calling were purely aesthetic. The lumberyard rated high on my list, and the owner, Mr. Alexander, knew that come Saturday, I was bound to show up. From a block away, I could hear the whine of his table saw as daily business was conducted. And the sound of the saw told me exactly what he was cutting. A steady *zip-zip-zip* meant an

order for laths; a sustained whirring meant planks were being processed; and if the saw started out on a high note and droned down the scale, I knew he was cutting two-by-fours.

While I was there, Mr. Alexander was content to let me roam at will. I always began my inspection in his office. It was a cramped little space, with two large windows that fronted on Main Street. The light that spilled through those windows splashed across walls covered with colored prints and calendar pictures.

Mr. Alexander was a Scotsman, and all the scenes depicted his Highlands. I never tired of viewing them. In fact, they were the sole reason I spent any time at all in the office. It was the inner reaches—the working depths of the lumberyard—that really drew me.

After leaving the lumberyard, I'd spend some time visiting the other businesses that held an interest for me. I'd roam the sporting goods department of Greenfield's Hardware Store, admiring the array of hunting equipment on display and fantasizing about what I could accomplish afield with the things I saw.

Similarly, I'd wander through Ludlow's Garage, inspecting the cars brought in for service or repair. If I was fortunate, Mr. Ludlow would let me sit behind the wheel of one so I could pretend to drive. It was great fun.

Making these rounds occupied the better part of a morning. And with them over, it was time to give serious consideration to having lunch.

Our clan reassembled at the car for the midday meal. The victuals came from a huge food basket Mom had packed the night before. Most everyone from out of town brought one, and by quarter after 12, the entire length of Main Street resembled a picnic site. Car trunks were opened, food was distributed, and people sat on fenders, bumpers and running boards while they ate. Fried chicken and potato salad was our usual fare, supplemented with soda pop and ice cream from the cafés.

After lunch, Mom did the grocery shopping at Crosby's General Store. Since these were the days before shopping carts, I was invariably recruited to assist. As Mom roved the aisles, making selections and checking them off a list, I'd carry the items to the front of the store and heap them on the counter. Then, when she was finished, I'd help tote the packed boxes and bags to the car. It wasn't hard work, not compared to some of the farm chores I had to do, and Mom always gave me a dime as reward. This money I channeled into the purchase of comic books. In those days they cost only a nickel apiece.

Al's Café had the best selection of comics in town. His establishment was also the bus stop, and to satisfy travelers, he stocked a good assortment of reading material. Part of his magazine display was one of those revolving racks that held the latest issues of Action Comics. My favorites were Tarzan, Red Ryder and Superman. But since I bought only two a week, the selection process took a while. Browsing was half the fun, and I often spent a couple of hours arriving at a final choice.

The rest of the afternoon I'd just drift, letting time take care of itself. I'd loll on the manicured lawn in front of the post office and read my comics. Most weekends I'd bump into friends from school. Invariably we'd end up at the ice-cream parlor, where, for a dime, we'd get the best chocolate sundaes west of Winnipeg.

As the afternoon waned, the family would gather again at the car for supper. It wasn't a picnic this time, however; supper meant eating at the Star Café. It was Dad's treat, and we could order whatever we wanted.

My choice was always the same: fish and chips. I loved the way Mr. Wong fixed them. He'd deep-fry fresh cod inside cocoons of crispy batter, and serve fist-sized chunks of this delicacy with homemade French fries and creamy coleslaw. Milk was the obligatory drink, and cherry pie the standard dessert.

After supper was social time for the older folks. People strolled Main Street, stopping to visit with friends. This was when the family car really came into its own. On Saturday nights, the automobile was accorded the same status as the parlor, and the calling process adopted the

mannerisms of a come-and-go tea. The ladies held court from the front seat and, one or two at a time, their friends would settle in the back to chat awhile before moving on to visit elsewhere.

Dad and the other men sat on benches near the cenotaph and talked about farming and politics. On occasion, they were even known to slip into the beer parlor for a cold draft. As for me, I went to the movies.

The Arcadia Theatre was run by Mr. Corns, and he screened two features a week. From Monday to Wednesday the films were romances, starring the likes of Claudette Colbert and Charles Boyer. My older sisters loved them.

Jawbreakers, jellybeans, gumdrops and a dozen other kinds of bulk candy filled trays inside.

On weekends, however, the bill of fare took a turn for the better, at least from my standpoint. It was then that Mr. Corns showed action pictures. They were guaranteed to please a juvenile audience, and my favorites were John Wayne Westerns, war movies and anything that had to do with pirates.

I liked to get to the Arcadia early. That way I could reserve a prime spot in the front row by leaving my jacket on the seat, and give myself plenty of time to purchase the goodies necessary to see me through the movie. These included a large Coke for a nickel, a jumbo box of popcorn for a dime and 10 red licorice whips at a penny apiece. Nine of the latter were for normal consumption. I bit the ends off the 10th and used it as a straw for drinking the Coke. Admission and treats cost 35 cents—a small price to pay for two hours of intense pleasure.

The show got out at 9 p.m., and as soon as it was over, I headed back to the car. The stores were open till 10, and as long as Main Street was lit, the adults were content to loaf and gossip. That gave me the chance to make one last excursion into Satler's Drugstore. I always held back a dime for this last-minute spree, and I always bought the same thing—jawbreakers. I'd get 100 of them for that single dime, and with judicious rationing, I could make them last from one Saturday until the next.

"Next Saturday …" When I was a kid, those words held magic. ❖

Downtown Shopping

By Marilyn Marquis Soules

R eturning from a shopping trip to the mall, I was reminded of the shopping trips to downtown Pittsburgh that my sister and I used to make with our parents, usually on Saturdays. Nowadays I might dash to the mall in sweats or jeans, but in those days, no lady, young or old, would be seen downtown without proper attire.

That being the rule, out would come the perfectly starched and ironed dresses, patent leather Mary Janes and, depending on the weather, the good winter or spring coat and hat, and the sign of every perfect little lady, the white gloves.

The trip might be made for school clothes and shoes, or it might be made to see a movie and stage show at the Stanley Theater.

Trips downtown always began the same way—with a ride on the "88" streetcar, which took us into the heart of the city. We would usually get started around 9 a.m., and it would take close to an hour to arrive at our destination.

First on the agenda would be selecting dresses (nobody wore pants to school in those days). Polly Flinders and Cinderella provided us with such a variety of colors and styles that it was difficult to decide, but with Mom's guidance, we were able to select a nice variety of dresses for the coming school year.

Next would come the purchase of the dreaded winter underwear. These were the heavy cotton-and-wool-blend panties and vests (which were sometimes itchy) for wear during the cold weather.

I was particularly unhappy about those serviceable, no-nonsense garments, and insisted on a supply of silk panties to wear over the sturdier ones. My mother's patience must have been infinite because she always indulged me in this,

Facing page: *Trolley* by Leo Stans, Courtesy of Wild Wings

and during winter I was always clad in two pairs of panties—one heavy and warm, and the other silky and much more to my liking.

Sometimes we had lunch at the tea room in one of the department stores. It was such fun to order from the children's menu and sip chocolate milk through a straw and pretend to be grown-up ladies having lunch together.

Sometimes, though, we stopped at a restaurant known as the Brass Rail. The ambience of the tea room was missing, but the aroma there was wonderfully redolent of hamburgers with frying onions. I've never had a hamburger to equal those served at the Brass Rail.

Streetcars like this one carried the author and her family to downtown Pittsburgh.

getting a well-deserved break from the two of us. She might read or visit with friends or just sit and enjoy the quiet and freedom from our little squabbles, which were usually caused by something like "Mom, she's looking at me!"

The Christmas windows were a delight, with every store attempting to outdo the others in presenting a Christmas fantasy. Some stores would designate five or six windows for the display and decorate them so that they told an entire fairy tale. Sleeping Beauty, Cinderella or Snow White would come to life as we walked from window to window. Some would even have "live" puppet shows with puppeteers working behind the scenes to portray Punch and Judy or one of the beloved tales from the Brothers Grimm.

What a wonderful time to be a child! With the promise of Christmas soon-to-be and the enchantment of the stories coming to life before our very eyes, we were certainly two very excited little girls by the time we settled in a booth at Stouffers for a snack. (I think this was part of Dad's strategy for settling us down for the ride home on the streetcar.)

It was always crowded and noisy and filled with people who worked downtown, as well as shoppers like us. The waitresses scurried from table to table, splendid in their maroon uniforms, each with a linen handkerchief adorned with beautiful lace peeking out of her breast pocket. Each delicate hankie was more beautiful and ornate than the last, as though there were a competition to see which waitress could wear the prettiest. Those waitresses must have been exhausted at the end of their shifts because the minute a table emptied, it would be immediately occupied by another group of hungry patrons.

The most fun trip downtown was during the Christmas season, when Dad would take us to see the animated window displays in the department store windows. We usually did this on a Sunday afternoon. Mom stayed home,

With Christmas on our minds, this was the time to let Dad know what we wanted Santa Claus to bring us, and to relive and discuss all the delightful things we had seen. We recited it all over again for Mom once we got home.

I miss those trips "downtown" in the days when shopping didn't have to be "convenient" and was leisurely fun.

The department stores have all relocated to the suburban malls or have closed their doors forever. The Brass Rail no longer exists, and the Christmas displays at the malls, although beautiful, will never equal the thrill of watching a puppet show or a whole fairy tale come to life. Wouldn't it be wonderful to be able to take a trip back in time to those childhood days when everything, even a simple shopping trip, was an adventure? ❖

Shopping in the 1950s

By Mary Louise Hopkins Billiot

I remember well the Good Old Days before shopping malls went up. We could go shopping in the city from store to store. The stores opened at 9:30 a.m., but the shoppers often arrived an hour before they opened, lining up in front of one particular store that was having a fantastic sale. Beautiful dresses that normally sold for $10–$25 would often be marked down to $5, and sometimes even $2. Everything in the store would be marked down to fantastic prices that today boggle the mind.

In this particular store everything was placed on tables. When the doors opened, everyone pushed and shoved to get to those tables, grabbing everything in sight. I don't think most of the women cared if the handfuls of items they grabbed fit them or not. The fun was seeing how much a person could grab without getting stomped and trampled—a real art, to say the least.

The real fun came when the ladies began to fight over an article.

Like going to a good sports game, the real fun came when the ladies began to fight over an article, pulling and ripping it before they could even see what size it was. It all seems rather humorous and pointless now, but when I was a teen-ager, it was the highlight of my month.

Of course, there were other stores to battle in, and I would tramp from one to another looking for incredible bargains. With $25, I often would come home with several new dresses, a pair of slacks, a pair or two of shoes, a couple of sports outfits, several pairs of socks, jewelry, a bag of candy and a bag of Planters Peanuts.

From store to store and from one end of the city to the other, I tramped for some needed—and some not so needed—items. Often, however, I bought little gifts for everyone in my family, something I have always really enjoyed.

The people in the Planters Peanuts shop always tried to lure the shoppers into their store. The Planters Peanuts man walked up and down the streets offering free samples of their delicious, hot-roasted, salted Spanish peanuts and cashews. To top it all off, the store kept its doors open and had a fan inside that kept the aroma of fresh-roasted peanuts floating throughout the area for the whole day. I just followed my nose to where I could buy a pound of Spanish peanuts for 35 cents.

Come noontime, I had to find a five-and-dime store and buy a turkey dinner, with coffee and pie a la mode, for $1.59. This was meeting-new-people time for me, and I conversed with other customers about all sorts of things.

We actually talked about current events and cultural topics. Though I was a teenager, I did not converse with only those who were my age; I really enjoyed talking to adults, also.

Once full of good food and good conversation, and having met many new friends, I was ready to hit the streets again and find the store that would have the perfect dress or outfit made especially for me.

This, of course, meant trying on dozens of dresses in dozens of different stores before I could actually find the right one. Woolworth's, Kresge's, Quackenbushes and J.C. Penney were just a few of the great name stores in which I shopped.

It probably was a good thing that the stores closed at 6 p.m., because I was exhausted by then and loaded down with bunches of bundles. While waiting for the bus to go home, I was always amazed at how much I could buy for just $25. But it was my own hard-earned money I had spent, earned from a paper route, baby-sitting, tutoring children and selling seeds and homemade pot holders.

The best part of the bus trip home was that usually tall, blue-eyed Hans, the German boy to whom I helped teach English, would be

casually sitting in the backseat with his feet up on the side of the seat in front of him.

Hans, the fine gentleman that he always was, would see me struggling with my packages while I tried to keep from being thrown into his lap. He then would ask me, "Would you like to have my seat?" As soon as anyone else would get off the back row, I would manage to ask the person sitting next to me to slide down so I could offer Hans a seat next to me.

His first question was always, "Well, what did you buy today?"

"Not much," I would answer, as I smiled and looked at my many packages. "Just some really great comic books, which, by the way,

I will gladly trade with you, come next Saturday, if you would be interested."

"Sure, why not?" he would answer. "Have some peanuts?"

"Sure, why not?" I would answer, feeling that my shopping excursion was highly successful and most satisfying indeed.

I always felt kind of sad that I would have to work for a couple weeks before going shopping again.

To be sure, I would be back again to battle the crowds, for what greater joy was there for a young teenager in those days than to go shopping and then ride home on the bus next to a handsome young man? ❖

Old Gold ad, House of White Birches nostalgia archives

"Satdays" Were the Best

By T.O. Pritchett

When I was growing up on the farm, Saturday was *the* day—the day around which it seemed our lives revolved. "Satday" was payday. Satday was the day everyone quit work at noon and headed for town. It was the day for seeing your friends, and it was the day for seeing your girl.

It was the day the stores stayed open until 9 p.m., and the day to do your shopping. It was the day for movies and popcorn, and the day for defeating your rival in a cutthroat game of pool.

I like to think we would have given up our trip to town if the neighbor's house had been on fire, but I'm glad we were never put to the test. Christmas and our birthdays were great events, but they only came once a year. Satday came every week.

The three blocks of the business section of Main Street were always lined with cars. Both sides of Main Street were filled with people strolling or standing, talking to friends. Just walking up the street and back took a long time because so many people wanted to talk.

Most of the women gathered in one of the two 10-cent stores, and the men ganged up on the corner or in the barbershop or pool hall. The barbershop was one of the busiest places in town.

On Saturdays the movies featured a Western, a comedy and a serial. Up until the early '30s, the films were silent. Most times there was a pianist playing music appropriate to the action on the screen. The kids ate popcorn and yelled encouragement to the hero. It cost a dime to get in, and popcorn was a nickel a bag.

For the grown-ups, the pool hall was where the action was. Some of the town boys fancied themselves pool sharks and saw the country boys as fish, and inveigled them into a game for money. Many times the country boys turned the tables and took the sharks. But most of the time it was just friendly rivalry between groups, and it carried over from week to week.

A lot of business was transacted in the poolrooms. During planting time or harvest, farmers came to the poolroom looking for help in the fields. Guns, watches and knives were traded, and information passed around. If you were looking for someone, the poolroom was a good place to start. And in bad weather, the pool hall offered warmth and companionship.

Satday was the day everyone quit work at noon and headed for town.

A lot of courting took place on Satdays, too. The movies were a good place to hold hands, and if your girl would promenade with you up and down Main Street or sit in a car and watch the other couples and talk, you felt like you were nine feet tall and would walk on air all the next week.

If you didn't want to go home for supper, you could get a hamburger or a hot dog for a dime at the poolroom's lunch counter. Or, in the winter, a big, hot bowl of chili was well worth the 15 cents it cost. If you were in the chips, you could go to the City Restaurant and get ham and eggs or liver and onions for 35 cents.

For dessert you could go to The Palace of Sweets, which featured marble-topped tables for four with woven wire chairs, ceiling fans and a long, marble-topped bar that dispensed huge malted shakes and sodas. I believe they only carried four or five flavors of ice cream, but that was enough. They also put out dainty cakes, cookies and pies. It was nearly always full of young people, especially on Satdays.

Now when we go downtown on Saturday nights, it is like going to a ghost town. The stores are dark, and the streets are empty. I always feel like humming that old song *Where Have All the Young Girls Gone?* or *Saturday Night is the Loneliest Night of the Week.* ❖

Town Days, Family Nights

By Nannie Tyson Ariola

We were raised on a farm and I was born in 1929, the seventh child of our family. We had very simple, hardworking and loving parents. Many of the things they taught us as children have helped us handle the trials and joys life has handed us.

We didn't have a car till my older brother joined the Navy in 1936. Everywhere we went we rode in a wagon pulled by Papa's team of work mules.

Saturdays were very special for us. Saturday mornings, we did our laundry on a rub board, using water from the well in the back yard and heated in the old black wash pot in the back yard.

But about noon, Papa hitched up the wagon while we all cleaned up and put on our best dresses. Then we went to town.

Mama and Papa always sat up on the wagon seat. When the weather turned bad and rain started, we stopped at a friend's house along the way till the shower passed. We children invented games along the way and enjoyed our trip.

The town was Carrollton, Texas. We pulled up behind the O.L. Dickerson General Store. Papa tied the team, and we went to do our shopping. We raised most of our supplies, but Papa bought what staples we needed on credit from one fall to the next, when our first bale of cotton was sold. It was the same at the dry goods store.

The old general store had barrels of pinto beans, pickles and all kinds of penny candy. It had an old-fashioned cash register and many things hanging on the wall. We children thought that store must be kind of like heaven. The smells made our little tummies turn over, we were so hungry. Papa usually bought a roll of bologna and some cheese and a big box of crackers, and—oh!—what a feast that was!

We girls saved our pennies all week if we got some from our older brother, and tied them in a corner of our handkerchiefs. Then we took a long time deciding on our penny candy. We usually bought a large, brown chocolate sucker called BB Bats. It lasted all the way home.

After Papa bought our groceries, we visited the pharmacy for our dishes of ice cream with

Family nights were spent around the radio listening to the *Grand Ole Opry* out of Nashville on WSM.

Mama's egg money. Then we went by the ice house and got 50 pounds of ice. We put it in a No. 3 washtub and covered it with cotton sacks. That was for our Saturday-night ice cream, frozen in our old, hand-cranked wooden freezer. We used that freezer for years.

The rest of the family usually came home for this. We'd listen to the *Grand Ole Opry* on our battery radio. (We never had electricity in our farm home.) This was our "Town Day," and "Family Night" came after the team was unhitched, fed and watered.

I'm 78, and these memories are dear to my heart still. ❖

Town Night

By Joyce Tintjer

The one event we all looked forward to, the high point of every week following six days of hard work on the family farm, was Town Night! Not only did we kids anticipate it, but Dad and Mom did, too. I know, because there were very few times that we missed Town Night. It was the one social event that broke up the monotony of everyday life.

But Town Night was also a necessity. We loaded the trunk of the family car with crates of eggs from our flock of Barred Rocks to trade for the grocery items we couldn't produce on our farm. Our destination was the small town of Baxter, in rural central Iowa.

I vaguely remember times when it rained while we were in town, making the dirt road back to our home an impassable quagmire. Then we would park the car along the road where the gravel ended and trudge the last half-mile home through the mud. (As the youngest of six children, I usually was carried by my dad or one of my teenage brothers, so it wasn't such an ordeal for me.) But Town Night was so important that even the threat of rain didn't stop us from going.

> *It was the one social event that broke up the monotony of everyday life.*

Once in town, Dad headed for the pool hall, Mom visited with the neighbor women at the mercantile, and we kids found our school friends to pal around with until the movie started. We each had 15 cents in our pockets—10 cents to get in and a nickel for candy or ice cream—and we thought we had the world by the tail.

Three or four of my girlfriends and I would link arms and stroll up and down Main Street, taking up most of the sidewalk. We didn't have too much to do with the boys, but we sure took notice of them. Usually the boys teased us, and we acted as though they were awful, but deep down we all liked the attention. Why else did we put on our best dresses, tie up our hair in bright ribbons, and sneak on a coat of bright red lipstick? Of course, we carefully wiped it off before our mothers caught us wearing it.

While we girls strolled the streets, patriotic march music blared from a loudspeaker. They always played the same numbers prior to the movie. Today, whenever I hear John Philip Sousa's *Stars and Stripes Forever*, I'm transported back to the days of my childhood, reliving Town Night.

As a small child, I was terrified of the dark. Carol, one of the girls I palled around with, told us about a certain building down one of the dimly lighted side streets from which a bogeyman would often emerge to pursue innocent victims. The decrepit building had a large opening in the front, and its interior was pitch black.

One night, Carol dared us to go down that street, and we apprehensively took her up on it. We didn't want to be called sissies. As we passed the gaping blackness of the building, she glanced back over her shoulder and shrieked, "Run! Here he comes!"

I was so convinced that I could feel the bogeyman's breath on my neck and sense his gnarled hands reaching out to drag me back into his lair. I'm sure I never ran faster in my entire life.

Of course there was no bogeyman, but just the same, from then on, we religiously avoided that particular street after dark.

The movie was the high point of Town Night. It was shown in a large hall above the mercantile. A small projection screen sat on a stage at the front of the hall. Folding chairs had been placed in neat rows to accommodate the moviegoers, with aisles left open down the center and on either side.

We saw the national news by way of the newsreels that always preceded the main feature. We also saw cartoons and, often, a serial. One long-running serial was *The Mummy's Hand,* a frightening tale about an Egyptian mummy who came back to life and haltingly pursued his victims while still partially wrapped in tattered strips of cloth.

Features such as these fed my childhood fears, but overall, the movies were great— except for the times we had to wait for the projectionist to splice the broken ends of the film. That happened on a regular basis.

Some of my favorite movies were the *Francis the Talking Mule* movies starring comedian Donald O'Connor, and the Westerns starring Roy Rogers and Dale Evans, Gene Autry and Randolph Scott.

Admission to the movies cost 10 cents for children and 35 cents for adults. My best friend, Doris, and I had shot up to almost adult height by age 11; she was 5 feet 8 inches, and I was just an inch shorter. The man who sold the tickets always suspiciously questioned us about our "real" ages when we handed over our dimes. Doris' mother was nearly at the point of sending along her daughter's birth certificate to end our harassment.

Doris told me teasingly that her mother was going to put bricks on her head to slow down her growth spurt.

For a brief time, cash prize drawings were held at the movies during intermission. We put our ticket stubs in a cardboard box with a slot cut in the top.

On one occasion, I was the lucky one, and I won $35 when my stub was drawn!

That was a colossal amount to a youngster growing up in the '40s and '50s.

Ice cream was a special treat. It came packaged in little cardboard tubs, and we ate it with a little wooden spoon. On the underside of each lid was a movie star's picture that we could peel off and save. We girls treasured these images of our favorite actors and actresses, and we collected and traded them among ourselves, just like baseball cards. If only I still owned my collection! It would probably be worth a large sum in our memorabilia-hungry society.

By the end of the evening, Mom had exchanged all the local gossip and we kids were getting sleepy. It had been a long evening. But Dad, down at the pool hall, rarely seemed to notice the late hour. Inevitably, Mom would send us kids to remind Dad of the time. We were actually allowed to go inside the pool hall. What a different era we lived in then!

Life was hard in the '40s and '50s, but we had few of the woes that plague modern society. It was a more innocent time. We enjoyed good, clean fun during the big social event of the week—Town Night. ❖

On the underside of each lid was a movie star's picture that we could peel off and save.

This photo of Cary Grant from the movie *Gunga Din* (1930) was from a Dixie Cup ice cream treat and was like those that the author collected.

Schrafft's

By Eileen Higgins Driscoll

W hy do you cut a sandwich in three pieces instead of in half like the other people do?" I asked my mother when I was about 10 years old. "Because that's the way Schrafft's does it," she replied. Growing up in Brooklyn during the Depression of the 1930s offered some special treats. One of the best was lunch at Schrafft's. Mother would say, "I think we will have lunch out today." I would jump with delight. In my mind, that meant Schrafft's.

We couldn't afford to go out to lunch very often, so it was always exciting. I would change into my Sunday clothes. (They were the clothes we had bought this year. Last year's clothes were school clothes, and older than that, the clothes were either given to a younger child or declared play clothes.)

> *We couldn't afford to go out to lunch very often, so it was always exciting.*

We would walk to Flatbush Avenue from our house, and for a nickel, we could ride the trolley to Church Avenue and Schrafft's. Oh, what fun! Nobody had built a mall, so Flatbush Avenue was lined with one interesting store after another. Most of the stores were privately owned.

Mother and I would saunter down the street, window-shopping. Block after block, the stores were bursting with good things for sale. There were shoe stores galore. Shoes were essentials, so even during the Great Depression, those stores seemed to do better than some of the others. I remember a big store that sold pianos. That was a luxury item, but I guess some people could afford one.

Each store window carried a feast for the eyes. Even if we couldn't buy anything, we could still enjoy looking.

When we arrived at the corner of Church and Flatbush avenues, we were greeted by the sight of

Lunch Counter by John Falter © 1946 SEPS: Licensed by Curtis Publishing

a beautiful church on the corner. (I'm sure that's how the street got its name.) The church's steeple towered over the other buildings. It also had a graceful set of steps that led up to elaborately carved wooden doors.

I am remembering back more than 60 years, but I believe there was a graveyard behind the church. It was a peaceful spot in the middle of the hustle and bustle of a busy city. The church was so old that it probably had been built before the big city of Brooklyn surrounded it.

We arrived at Schrafft's after a short walk. The window that faced Flatbush Avenue showed beribboned and red-velvet–covered boxes of chocolates. There were also some less expensive, shiny black-and-white boxes of chocolates. Husbands, boyfriends and suitors brought them to their ladies fair for Valentine's Day, birthdays, anniversaries and other celebrations.

When we opened the glass doors to the restaurant, we stepped onto a large tiled marble floor. A counter ran along one side. Marble- and wood-topped tables with ice-cream-parlor chairs were arranged on the floor. The chairs had round seats with heavy wire backs styled in a scroll design. They were not very comfortable, but they sure were pretty.

The waitress wore a black dress with a white tea apron, and a small white cap. She brought water, a napkin and silverware with the menu. That was much more fun than setting the table for family meals at home.

Deciding what to order was a big problem. What was in the sandwich didn't matter as much as the fact that I was eating out. The second most important thing was whether to order an ice-cream soda or an ice-cream sundae. And when that decision had been made, another popped up: What flavor? Once that monumental decision was made, I could relax. I took small spoonfuls so it would all last a little longer.

Little did I know what wonderful memories Mother and I were making at the time. I had Mother alone for a time, and we had a very special lunch together. Schrafft's will always carry a special memory for me. ❖

Lunch at Woolworth's

By John Dinan

One of the great trials for a 1930s kid was the obligatory trip downtown on Mom's shopping day. One of the great joys, however, was lunch at Woolworth's. The lunch counter that ran down one side of the store served a meal fit for a queen (and her kid).

Imagine a complete roast turkey dinner—including dressing, gravy, fresh vegetable, whipped potatoes and a hot roll with butter—for 25 cents. Soups were a dime, as were the desserts, and if you were lucky, you could get a jumbo banana split for a penny.

The Woolworth stores were usually located near a bus line so it was most convenient on those weekly shopping trips. As there were no fast-food chains, Woolworth's lunch counters were one of very few downtown lunch options.

A great variety of meals were offered, each pictured on a long line of signs high above the back of the lunch counter. Breakfast specials could be had for a few cents, and a simple

hot-dog-and-Coke combination and tuna-salad sandwich were similarly low priced. A complete meal could be had for less than a quarter.

No small part of the Woolworth's lunch counter experience was spinning around in the chair. After a few such spins and a few admonitions from Mom, I would settle down for a treat of my choice, which in itself was a novel experience for a kid then. Eating what *I* decided on the spot—that was something!

Up to the late 1960s, the Woolworth lunch counter was one of the few breakfast/lunch games in town. Between 1970–1995, fast-food restaurants proliferated, as did the mobility of the average family, which was no longer captive to the city's downtown business district. Thus continued the demise of the Woolworth five-and-dime and its fabulous lunch counter.

They are all gone now, but not forgotten by those of us who remember the one high spot of that downtown shopping trip with Mom. ❖

Soda-Fountain Delights

By John L. Patton

The one icon from my growing-up days in the mid-1950s is the drugstore soda fountain, complete with swivel stools. In those days, youngsters and oldsters alike spent many pleasant moments relaxing with friends while enjoying soft drinks and ice-cream sodas in a festively lit corner of the local drugstore.

My pals and I had our drinks along with a plate of potato chips served with a side dish of ketchup for dipping, a treat I still enjoy today.

The Kenross drugstore in the Cincinnati neighborhood of Fairmount where I grew up was our favorite. We could read their comic books as we sipped our phosphates. And we liked their phosphates since they used two extra squirts of flavoring for a stronger taste.

For those who don't remember, a phosphate was made by filling the bottom of a soda glass with fruit flavoring or chocolate syrup and then adding seltzer water. It was really a soda without the ice cream, and it sold for 15 cents less than a three-scoop soda. They'd add shaved ice if you asked, and then you could eat it with a spoon. That's the way I liked mine.

Of course, they had a menu thumb-tacked to the wall listing all the tasty treats they made: short and tall sodas, small and large sundaes, half- and full-sized banana splits, dishes and cones of ice cream, malts and milkshakes, and the phosphates. The flavorings were lemon, lime, cola, grape, chocolate (with or without a spoon of malt powder added) and cherry. Toppings included chopped nuts, plain or salted; crushed pineapple, strawberry, hot fudge, butterscotch and chocolate jimmies. They all came with whipped cream and a cherry on top.

Kenross offered a few treats you could get nowhere else, making for loyal customers. The owner's wife baked molasses cookies and brownies most every afternoon, and topped them with a scoop of butterscotch sauce and a good-sized squirt of whipped cream. I saved my allowance or ran errands so I could enjoy a few of Mrs. Kenross' creations each week. Those molasses cookies were especially good.

Mrs. Kenross was always behind the soda fountain to greet my friends and me after school every day, but they hired a high-schooler for Saturdays and Sundays. I dreamed of working there when I was old enough, but we moved away too soon. That was only one of the many reasons I protested when I found out we were going to a new neighborhood.

Drugstores weren't the only place soda fountains could be found, as this illustration from a 1950s Pullman railroad car ad proves.

Mrs. Kenross, a short, stout woman with long golden hair, always asked us what we had learned in school and expected each of us to tell her something interesting. When we got our report cards, she wanted to see them, and if we had done well enough, she would put an extra cookie or brownie in the dish when she made us one of her special treats. If we hadn't gotten a good report card, she always encouraged us to try a tad bit harder. In exchange for our oath to buckle down, we'd get a single-scoop cone.

Mrs. Kenross was my favorite adult for a long time—and not just because of her soda-fountain treats. ❖

The Monterey Bus

By Bonnie Moyers

Back in the 1950s, when I was a child, we lived in the country, about three miles west of the nearest small town, Churchville, Va., and about 12 miles from the nearest city, Staunton, Va. My mother was a stay-at-home mom who didn't drive. But if we needed to go shopping or to a doctor or dentist, we didn't usually have to ask Dad to take off work to drive us. We had a measure of independence thanks to a bus that ran from Monterey, Va., to Staunton and back.

I became acquainted with the Monterey bus as a child. The bus was medium-sized, smaller than a Greyhound or Trailways. Since I was just a kid, I didn't pay much attention to the color, make or model of the bus, but I do recall that it was easy to catch. We simply stood at the edge of the highway in front of our home. The driver would slow down, stop and pick us up.

The bus ran regularly, leaving Monterey early each morning. It headed east on Route 250, picking up passengers along the route, until it reached the Greyhound-Trailways station in Staunton. Everyone got off there.

The departure of the Monterey bus was the end of a very special era.

Some passengers took taxis to other parts of town. But Mama, my little brother, David, and I walked farther downtown. That's where we transacted most of our business. If we had a doctor appointment, we went to the Professional Building to see Dr. Campbell, our general practitioner. Dr. Pemberton, the eye doctor, also had his office there. Farther up Frederick Street, in a lovely old renovated private home, Dr. Bradford, our pediatrician, and his nurse, Miss Johnson, saw their patients.

When we had our teeth checked, drilled or filled, we paid a visit to Dr. Gilbert in the Industrial Loan Building across the street, riding the elevator to his office on the fourth floor. We could get prescriptions filled at Central Drugs on the corner.

When we were in town for the day, we usually did medical appointments and prescription filling in the mornings, because you never knew how long those might take. And we certainly didn't want to run the risk of missing our bus ride home!

We generally ate lunch either at Central Drugs or at the Woolworth's lunch counter, which was one street away, on West Beverley, Staunton's main street.

At the drugstore we usually had soup and sandwiches. At the lunch counter we could get soup and sandwiches, or a hot plate special. Usually we drank milk, but sometimes we were treated to a soda. If we didn't have a soda, we might have a candy bar or ice cream at the drugstore, or a piece of pie, cake or a doughnut at Woolworth's. Eating out was a great treat for us!

If there was enough time, we went shopping downtown. There were always things we needed—sewing notions, a new paring knife, school supplies, simple toiletries and cosmetics. We could find all those things and more at Woolworth's or the other two dime stores, McCrory's and Newberry's.

I think Mama enjoyed looking at everything just as much as we did, from the latest toys and clothes and gadgets to the live pets at the back of the stores.

Although we never bought a pet, we enjoyed looking at the turtles, fish, hamsters, gerbils, birds, puppies and kittens. It was one more thing that made our day special!

Sometimes we came to town only to shop, such as when we were shopping for school clothes or shoes. We went shopping at J.C. Penney's, Montgomery Wards, Leggetts (now called Belk) or the Carroll House.

There were other interesting places downtown, too—other clothing shops, one or two men's shops, a shoe repair place, two other drugstores, a couple of banks, Finkel's Furniture, two hardware stores and a bar that we didn't patronize.

We usually started walking back to the bus station about 3 or 3:30 p.m. so we would get there in time. Even little David helped carry smaller bags or packages.

Once there, we sat down to rest until the driver started up the bus. Just to make sure that nobody missed the bus, our driver would call,

Window Shopping by Ron DelliColli, House of White Birches nostalgia archives

"All aboard!" from the station doorway. Then we all climbed back aboard for the ride home.

I don't remember exactly how much it cost to ride the bus. I do know that the fare was low enough that Mama never had to use a dollar bill. She always paid with pocket change. I recall her and Dad saying that the bus fare was very reasonable.

The Monterey bus could also be used as a connecting bus to get us to the station where we would board one of the buses to Richmond, Baltimore, or other distant cities.

When I was about 13, the Reynolds Bus Lines of Clarksburg, W.Va., retired the Monterey bus. Rumor had it that the kindly, helpful driver wanted to retire. We also heard that the customer base had shrunk. That was probably true, for by this time, more people owned their own vehicles.

I was sorry when the bus went. I would miss watching the scenery pass through its big windows, relaxing on the soft, thick, plush seats as the bus rolled along. I even missed the *chuff-chuff* of the brakes. The departure of the Monterey bus was the end of a very special era. And it was harder for us to arrange transportation thereafter.

Now I wish that I'd learned the bus driver's name. I also wish that I had obtained a picture of the bus.

I have owned and driven cars and trucks for many years now. But the Monterey bus will live on in my memory because it made possible the days that I've described here, days we enjoyed. That bus was one of my favorite forms of transportation on wheels while I was growing up. ❖

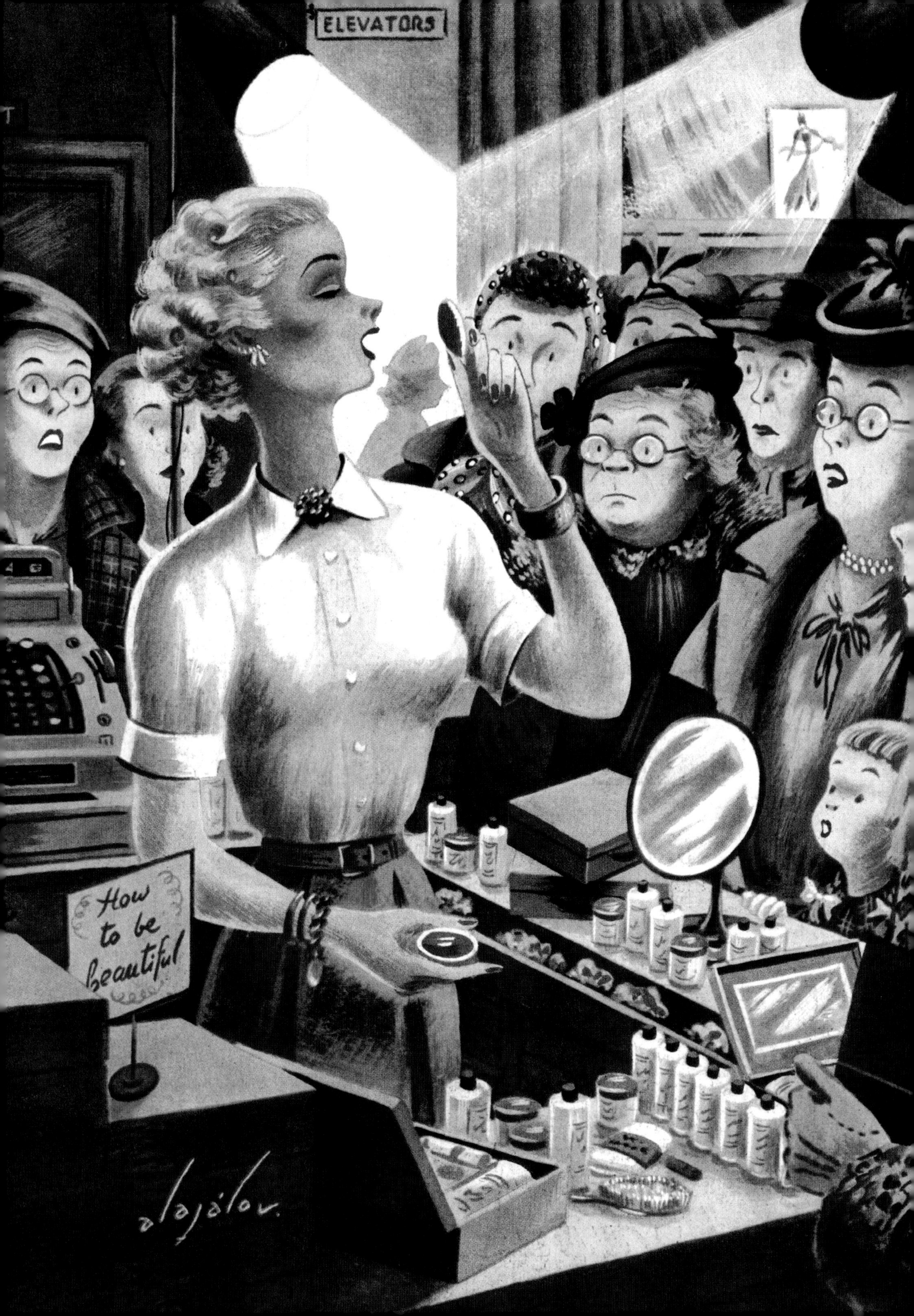
ELEVATORS
How to be beautiful
alajálov.

Trade Nights

By Dorothy Rieke

During one recent week, my husband and I traveled from our farm to town at least five times for repairs, groceries and other necessities. Most of those trips were hurried and not especially memorable. However, during the 1930s, it was customary for farmers and their families to travel only once a week to the nearest town to trade their eggs and cream for groceries. Indeed, at that time, those Saturday-night trips were anticipated, greatly enjoyed and long remembered.

Farmers labored every weekday from dawn to darkness. But Saturday nights were special, and nearly everyone looked forward to a trip to town on "trade night."

After arriving in town and leaving the produce at the general store, Dad drove along Main Street searching for a parking place. Because it took time to test cream and candle eggs, Mother always shopped before trading for groceries.

Sis was anxious to locate her girlfriends. Together they would spend the evening inspecting stylish floral print dresses in the department store, admiring sparkling rhinestone jewelry at Woolworth's and flirting with our neighbor's sons. At my age, I thought boys were a waste of time because while the boys discussed field work and horses, the girls nervously giggled.

I always regarded trips to town as wonderful adventures. Tantalizing glimpses of store offerings frequently triggered my vivid imagination. I saw myself wearing the stylish dresses, large flowered hats and high-heeled sandals—or parading around in one of those pink housecoats. I just *knew* the future would bring everything I ever wanted.

One of my favorite places was the corner drugstore with its soda fountain. Inside the door of that store was a white, counterlike machine. The tantalizing aroma of heated cashews, pecans, peanuts, almonds and walnuts in a revolving lazy susan greeted everyone. Once I spent 25 cents at that counter to buy about 3 tablespoons of nuts. As much as I enjoyed those, I never made that financial error again. But my mouth often watered at the thought of those rich, salty nuts.

Makeup Counter by Constantin Alajalov © 1951 SEPS: Licensed by Curtis Publishing

Farther back in this store, customers sat on high stools at a marble counter facing a large mirror where they gazed at their reflections or watched the soda jerk preparing sodas, malts, sundaes, cherry phosphates and other fountain delights. Nearby were round tables and wire chairs where groups could eat and visit.

Even though I was not allowed to use cosmetics, I was drawn to that counter where flat pink-and-gold Lady Esther powder boxes and lipsticks vied for my attention with midnight-blue-and-silver Evening in Paris gift boxes filled with perfumes, colognes and scented powders.

Another counter exhibited glittering gold and silver filigree-framed mirrored trays holding beautifully shaped embossed glass perfume containers, each capped with an eye-catching stopper. I desperately wanted one of those sets, but like many other things, they were far beyond the reach of a Depression girl.

Occasionally, while Mother shopped, Dad and I walked to the Pioneer Theater. As I studied colorful action posters of the current Western movie scenes, Dad purchased a 25-cent ticket for himself and a 10-cent ticket for me.

After locating seats in the theater, we joined the crowd yelling and clapping as Johnny Mack Brown or Wild Bill Elliot, dressed in fancy button-decorated shirts, fought gunfighters.

With their shopping completed, people stood in the streetlight-dotted darkness to discuss the hot weather, Roosevelt's New Deal and family matters. No one seemed in a hurry to go home.

Finally, when our family returned to the car, Dad reluctantly started it and backed out of the parking space. Sometimes he surprised us with a nickel bag of crisp, salted popcorn that he had purchased from the lady who sold it from a small street stand. As we headed home, everyone talked about the day's events.

We lived for those long-ago Saturday nights. They represented not only a respite from the labor and hardships of the '30s, but also a time when dreams of another world were spun, a world infinitely more exciting and glamorous than our world of failed banks and dry weather. Usually those glimpses of this other world were fleeting, but they were enough to sustain us for another week—until the excitement of the next Saturday night in town. ❖

Shopping Days

By Ruth Bousman

I can recall very vividly what it was like to shop many, many years ago. In the department stores of Grand Rapids, Mich., when a customer made a purchase, the clerk would put a ticket with the money in a little metal box, which would travel on a ceiling track to the main office.

Before long, back would come the little box with the sales ticket and the change. As a little girl, I always enjoyed watching the tiny metal boxes travel their route like tiny trains.

Back in those days, there were clerks behind almost every counter or two. One did not have to look very far to get questions answered or to find a certain department. There were also men on every floor—"floor walkers"—and they also answered questions.

I especially remember the elevator operators. No customer pushed the buttons and opened the elevator. This was done by a uniformed person who called out the various wares of every floor as the elevator stopped to let someone out or in.

It was fun to use the elevators and listen to the operators recite the various items for sale. As I remember, the elevators were always very crowded. Sometimes, they seemed to go down very fast, and my tummy did flip-flops!

Grocery stores permitted customers to charge food items. During the Depression years, my father made regular payments on the grocery bill.

The store owner would always give my father a small bag of candy "for the girls" every time he made a payment.

Back then, there were not long lines at checkout counters. Most stores delivered orders that had been phoned in or purchased in person. Every large store had its own delivery trucks with its name inscribed on the side panels.

We have more choices now, but the personal touch is somewhat diminished. We are no longer waited on—we mostly wait on ourselves. Sometimes I miss that personal touch of the Good Old Days! ❖

Shop 'Til We Drop

By Randi Ryan

As a grade-schooler, I was a city kid for most of the year. Back in the 1940s, folks who lived in the Bay Ridge neighborhood of Brooklyn, N.Y., were much more homebound than people usually are today. We walked everywhere. Moms did their shopping almost every day.

I often accompanied my mom on her shopping rounds. Pushing my baby sister in a carriage, we walked to the nearby business district where there was a grocery, a fruit-and-vegetable man, a butcher, a bakery, and a "candy store" where dads bought the morning paper on their way to the subway for the 30- to 40-minute commute to work.

Our subway station was on 69th Street in Bay Ridge, just a few blocks from both the Staten Island Ferry and our apartment home between 71st and 72nd on Colonial Road.

I knew that shopping run as well as Mom did. I can still picture the greengrocer, with his bristly, black mustache, his cheery way of joking with customers in his rolling Italian accent, and his big white apron that picked up his handprints after he broke the greens off the carrots and beets. Sometimes he gave me a little carrot to munch on—yum! Mom bought those and more—yellow or white turnips, cabbage, a batch of potatoes.

She'd plan it out so as not to buy everything at once. That would be too heavy a load, and we still had to stop at the butcher. He had helpers and a high glass case and lots of saws and blades for cutting meat on massive butcher blocks. Most of the meat was cut to order, though the noise from the meat grinder made it hard to shout loud enough so he could hear. He was a burly, smiling, grandfatherly fellow with a white mustache. He didn't talk much to kids.

I stood quietly by Mom, swirling circles in the sawdust on the wooden floor with my feet while he sliced bacon and wrapped stew beef. Everything was wrapped in paper in those days, and shoppers put the parcels in their own bags.

It was time to move on, with a quick stop at the greeting-card store so Mom could return her library book. The pay library gave you a three-day loan for a small fee—a quarter, I think—and Mom, who was an avid reader, usually had books coming and going.

Onward we went to the bakery across the street, our final stop, for whole wheat bread, or rye, and something for a treat with after-dinner coffee.

I can still picture the greengrocer, with his bristly, black mustache.

Mom spoke Norwegian with the staff while choosing a few éclairs or a seven-layer chocolate cake, or maybe Napoleons, or Danish pastries with apricot filling.

The lady tended to my priorities: "Would you like a cookie, dear?"

Of course I would! "Yes, thank you," I answered politely, and she passed me a small, buttery treat edged with chocolate.

Of course, I murmured my polite thank-you in Norwegian; I was in the habit of switching back and forth in this multilingual, multiethnic corner of the metropolis. Our neighborhood was a broad mix of German, Irish and Nordic. My childhood girlfriends covered a varied spectrum, and we hopscotched together in English.

Finally we were ready to be on our way, tired from all the walking and toting and visiting and shopping. It was time for us to head home for lunch. I hoped for canned tomato soup and grilled cheese, my favorite, and looked forward to tomorrow and our next trip to the shops! ❖

The Piano Lady

By James A. Nelson

I was one lucky 12-year-old. Dad had just informed me that Aunt Verna, his sister, was moving back to Spokane. Why was this such a break for a 12-year-old? Because she was my favorite aunt as well as The Piano Lady—not a piano salesman, but one fantastic piano player. She made a living playing at music stores and other places that sold sheet music. This was fairly common from the 1930s into the early 1950s.

"She will live with us, Jimmy, until she finds a job and gets her own place," Dad explained.

His words sent a warm feeling coursing through me. This meant that our Sunday family sing-alongs would commence once more. That was something a lot of families did many years ago.

I'm not sure what was more important: the joyful music that echoed from our living room on Sundays, or the family bonding that took place as our voices melodiously struggled with *I'm Looking Over a Four-Leaf Clover* and *Three Little Fishes Swimming Over the Dam.*

Aunt Verna had played in a small band that Bing Crosby had formed.

Thank goodness there was no television; had there been, I might not have such warm memories to occupy my "nostalgic moments," as I call them.

World War II was on. With so many men gone to war, jobs were easy to find, and it wasn't long before Aunt Verna landed one. I remember how excited she was when she burst through our door one morning with the big news. "Jim," she exclaimed to my dad, "I got a wonderful job at J.J. Newberry's. I'm going to be their piano lady!"

Many of us still remember the Newberry's downtown. This five-and-ten was the focal point of many towns in the United States. It was the only store that many families shopped at in those days—out of necessity for some and out of pure pleasure for others. It was the first place I headed with my birthday and Christmas gift money.

The big day finally arrived, and Aunt Verna headed downtown to start her new job. As she went out the door, my voice trailed after her, "I'll be downtown later, Aunt Verna, to hear you play."

She turned and smiled. "Thanks," she said, "and be sure to bring a crowd. I will need an audience."

At that time, Bing Crosby was a rising singing star—or "crooner," as he was called—in Hollywood. In my mind, Hollywood was the home of Mickey Mouse, that "wascally wabbit" Bugs Bunny, Porky Pig and the Wizard of Oz.

It was a magical place in California where the sun always shone and millionaire movie stars drove around in convertibles on yellow brick roads, heading for parties on the beach. At least that's what I believed.

Years before, Aunt Verna had played the piano in a small band that Bing Crosby had formed in Spokane.

Dad often talked about Bing and the others coming over to the house to practice. *Just imagine*, I thought, *Aunt Verna has actually played with Bing Crosby*! Could there have been anything greater than *that*?

Later that morning, Mom packed me a sack lunch and gave me 10 cents for cotton candy. In a flash I was out the door, heading for the emporium that held everything a little boy could desire—including The Piano Lady, Aunt Verna.

As I came through the door at Newberry's, I could hear the tinkling piano and her vibrant voice singing *Don't Fence Me In*. Bing Crosby had just taken that song to number one on the *Lucky Strike Hit Parade*, a popular Sunday radio show.

I worked my way through the crowd that had gathered around the sheet music area, hoping Aunt Verna would play my favorite song, the one that always ended our Sunday singalongs—*Bumble Boogie*. When she played that song, I couldn't help but dance. And often, we all did.

Finally making it to the front of the crowd, I stood blissfully swaying against the rope barricade, smiling and thinking, *This is my aunt, The Piano Lady*. As her music bounced from the front of the store to the back, the crowd grew even larger.

She finally got a break and asked me if I would like a cherry Coke at the soda fountain. She only had to ask once. I proudly took her hand so I could help her negotiate the large crowd. After all, she was my aunt as well as The Piano Lady.

After finishing our Cokes, I walked her back to the piano and gave her a warm hug. It was time for me to go. As I left the store, I heard someone ask, "Can you play *As the Caissons Go Rolling Along*? I have a son in the Army overseas."

"Of course," Aunt Verna replied warmly, "and I'll play it loud enough so he can hear it." That made me smile. ❖

B-Flat Daydreams

By Marlys Bradley Huffman

When you grew up on a farm, a trip to town was an excursion, but a trip to the city was a rare and special event. In our case, the city was Portland, Ore., and to me, the highlight of the trip was going to the music department of Portland's largest department store.

Instead of CDs and digital players, the music department featured instruments, lesson books and the latest in music. In one corner, a grand piano sat on a small, elevated platform and a talented lady spent the day playing all the newly published songs.

The platform was surrounded by racks of music. Interested listeners would hand one of the new issues of music to the sales clerk who handed it to the piano player. Soon she would play the selection and the customer would decide whether or not to buy it.

New editions of sheet music often had covers bearing the picture of the popular artist who had introduced the tune.

My mother would leave me at the music department while she made her other purchases. Standing there, I would imagine that I could play the music myself. Listening to the piano was all the treat I needed, but the day I was allowed to actually *buy* a piece of sheet music was fraught with both joy and agony.

First I had to decide which piece I really wanted. Then I had to find the courage to hand it to the salesgirl and ask to have it played. Should I choose *Harbor Lights* because I liked the song, or the piece with my favorite singer's picture on the cover? I had to decide before my mother returned; there could be no dawdling when Mother was ready to go. If I hadn't completed my purchase, I could expect to go home without anything.

World War II and gas rationing curtailed our trips to the city. Now the music department is a place of CD players, CDs, headphones and music cards. There's no place for a child to stand and daydream. ❖

Small Town Saturday

By Barbara Hudson

*I*n 1952, at the age of 17, I left our small West Texas town and the farm where I had been born and raised. But no matter how old I grow or how much of the world I experience, in my heart I will always be a country girl from Small Town, U.S.A. Life was slower, more relaxed in those early days, and my early life left vivid impressions to call upon from time to time. My earliest memories date back to the early 1940s, when most of our family still lived at home.

Residents of the town and surrounding farming communities were hardworking, God-fearing people. They labored Monday through Friday, but when Saturday rolled around, unless there was an emergency, they were ready to socialize and enjoy the day. Everyone from Grandma to the youngest child went to town on Saturday.

Our town was the county seat, and the courthouse was the hub of activity. The streets there form an exact square around the courthouse, and stores and businesses line the streets. On our Saturday trips to town, the prime parking places were right on the courthouse square.

One other event could change our Saturday ritual: the carnival's arrival.

Once the family vehicle was in position, the day's activities could begin. Frequently the occupants chose to simply sit for a while and watch the people walk by. Most of us diligently practiced people watching almost to the point of making it an art form. Eventually, though, individual family members would leave the vehicle to pursue the activity of choice.

The men usually migrated to the barbershop whether or not they needed a haircut, or they gathered in small groups on a corner, or sat on car fenders to discuss the week's events. The ladies leisurely shopped and caught up on the latest gossip, or possibly arranged for a visit during the week to exchange fruit or vegetables for canning, or to try out a new quilt pattern. Quilting bees were popular in those days.

For the children from about age 9 and up, Saturdays were very special indeed. The kids were free to wander around the square with their friends, have refreshments in one of the two drugstores, and maybe even catch the latest film at one of the three movie theaters.

It usually depended on how much money you could talk Dad out of, or your earnings from the week's chores. With 50 cents in your pocket you could have a great day—ice cream or a cherry Coke cost a nickel, and the movie was only a dime. Most kids stayed through the movie at least twice—that was *really* getting your money's worth.

The very old and the very young usually remained in the car. People would stop by and visit with them just as if they were at home.

The car was home base and everyone reported in periodically. It wasn't much of a system, but it worked fine. I don't recall ever losing a single family member—well, not for long.

A lot of good, clean flirting took place on Saturdays, too. Frequently the older girls (or boys) would get Cokes or ice cream from the drugstore and then just hang around the car, waiting for the "heartthrob of the week" to happen by.

But they would wait just so long, and if the object of their affection did not show up, they would casually stroll around the square, checking the regular hangouts. The idea was to find the unlikely love interest before he or she went to the afternoon movie with someone else! My first kiss from my first real boyfriend took place at the Saturday matinee.

In the fall, when it was time to harvest the crops, the Saturday festivities had an added feature. Then the town overflowed with farm workers who came to help harvest the crops—and we all participated in the original mass garage sale, or flea market. A couple of empty lots a block north of the square made a perfect place to set up. After cleaning out our closets and storage areas to find salable items, in no time at all, we were in business.

The empty lot quickly filled with racks of clothing and tables of goods. Usually two people stayed at the sale site, alternating during the day. I loved to stay and help my mother, as did many of my friends. We would run back and forth, checking to see who had sold the most. If we sold most or all of our goods in one day, that was terrific; if not, we brought them back the next Saturday.

One other event could change our Saturday ritual drastically: the carnival's arrival. Talk about people being excited! There was something wonderfully magical and mysterious about the carnival.

Aside from the bearded lady and the sword swallower, there were people the likes of which we had never seen before—very pretty women with very blond hair, wearing more makeup and less clothing than considered proper; and

there were adults who were smaller than children, and others who were giants!

Oh, and of course, there were rides—the Ferris wheel, the merry-go-round, the Tilt-A-Whirl (my favorite), and the hammer, which scared the daylights out of most people.

Besides all this, there were games where you could win prizes; the sideshows, some not considered morally fit; and best of all, the cotton

Soda Fountain Memories by Ron DelliColli, House of White Birches nostalgia archives

candy and snow cones. It was indeed an extra-special time when the carnival came to town.

When Saturday drew to a close and it was time to gather the family and head for home, no matter what variety of Saturday we had experienced, there was a lot of conversation about the day's events. Everyone had a story to tell.

But the evening chores were waiting for us. Then we would have supper and prepare for church on Sunday morning. There would be more socializing the next day—and the preacher might even join us for Sunday dinner. ❖

JOHN FALTER

Our Urban Delight

By Wynne Crombie

For the World War II-era child, the downtown department store was the magical place that contained a toy department. Ours was the Rhodes Department Store and it was in Tacoma, Wash. This urban delight issued its own credit card long before Visa or MasterCard. Our Rhodes card was the family's only credit card, and it was diligently paid off every month.

"Hon," my dad yelled to my mother on the first of every month, "where's the Rhodes bill?"

The department store of the 1940s had departments that no longer exist. I loved wandering into Rhodes' book department, where a Nancy Drew or a Hardy Boys was 75 cents.

The notions department was hidden away in a corner of the first floor. My mother shopped there for dress shields (do they sell those anymore?). She could also pick up pins, buttons, tape measures and scissors. In a child's eyes, it definitely did not spell excitement. In cahoots with the notions, but for some odd reason on a different floor, was the fabric department.

Then, as now, the men's department was on the first floor. There wasn't much variety. Everything seemed to be white—handkerchiefs, shirts, boxer shorts. Ties came in sensible colors, except at Christmas.

Women's wear tended to be more elaborate, but still sensible. But woe to the tall or petite; there were no special sizes.

Rhodes had a music department where, for $1, you could buy a record album. Sheet music was a big item; a willing clerk would even pump out the melody for prospective buyers on an old upright.

The most fascinating department for girls was the children's shoe department. We would try on a pair of shoes (always oxfords) and put our feet into a machine. A window at the top gave us a skeletal view of our feet. *Awesome!*

Paying for purchases was an exacting process. My mother would hand over her Rhodes card (or cash) to the clerk. The bundle was placed in a drive-in-bank-style cylinder. A button was pushed and the things *whooshed* upward to some hinder department where such things were taken care of. The reverse process—with the receipt in the cylinder—took place a few minutes later.

The revolving front door didn't come to Rhodes until the 1950s. When it did, we kids would go around and around until some adult came along to show us the error of our ways.

The Bon Marche in Seattle had an escalator long before Rhodes did—*wow, moving stairs*—but Rhodes had an elevator. The white-gloved elevator operator moved us from floor to floor by turning a big golden wheel. Most notable was her trill, "Up car, gooooing up." When she overshot a floor, she would say, "Oops," and get us back on track. She always knew everything about every floor and dutifully recited their contents.

Christmas was something else. The store would be open late, and after dinner we would troop into the car and head off for our department store Christmas odyssey. An electric train whizzed above us on a monorail. Toys would be divided into two camps: cars, truck and trains for the boys, and dolls, dollhouses and play stoves for the girls. Games and puzzles would sort of overlap into both sexes. And Santa would be there, clucking over all of us and asking if we had been good. But just to be sure, we always pointed out to our parents what we wanted.

Rhodes had no restaurant or food court—just a soda fountain on the mezzanine, where you could get the best hot fudge sundae ever.

There are numerous Marshall Fields, Lord & Taylors, and Nordstroms, but there was only one Rhodes. Long gone, it's now only a distant memory, but a happy one. ❖

The Shopping Trip

By Carole Hosey

The wonder of that first shopping trip isn't that it impressed me at a tender age; it doesn't take much to impress a 4-year-old. Rather, it is that more than a half-century later, after a full and exciting life, the smallest details of that simple expedition are still stored in my memory. Until that day, my world had been limited to my home, my grandparents' home and Sunday school. Then, on this memorable occasion, I entered an enthralling new world: Mama took me downtown.

Since my mother didn't drive, daytime outings were made by public transportation. My heart thudded when the varnished yellow wooden streetcar came around the curve of the street, blue sparks dancing between its power pole and the overhead wires.

I grasped Mama's hand tighter than ever. The streetcar wheels squealed as they ground to a stop at our corner, the door folded open and the steps unfolded down—all by themselves!

I was permitted to drop the coins into the small, glass-fronted fare box.

I was permitted to drop the coins into the small, glass-fronted fare box. Then, as the motorman rang the bell and pulled the lever to start the car, we chose our seats.

The pale, honey-colored, woven cane seats were smooth and slippery. Mama delighted me by pulling one of the seat backs forward so we could sit facing one another and each have a window seat. I pressed close to the open barred window. The wind blew against my face and the scenery flew past as we rocked along through the quiet, green residential streets into the center of town.

The main corner of town frightened me, too. It was crowded with people and noisy with honking cars and huge, rattling beer wagons with metal-rimmed wheels, pulled by enormous, snorting horses whose fringed hoofs sparked when they clattered across the streetcar tracks.

The heat from the brick street sizzled up my bare legs as Mama hurried me along, across the street and into the dusty shade of the green canvas store awnings, which sheltered a few squatting Indians and their wares.

We pushed with a gentle rush of air through the revolving doors, into the cool hush of Doerflinger's, the town's only department store. There was no canned music, no carpeted floors, no mirrored escalators of today's department stores, but it was spectacular to my childish eyes! Paddle fans twirled softly in the ceiling. The highly polished wooden floors creaked with our footsteps, and the pneumatic change-carrier capsules *ping-ping-ping*-ed as they rocketed along on overhead tracks from the departments to the bookkeeper in the office and back again.

While my mother selected a pair of kid gloves, I stood at her knee, round-eyed and gaping, entranced by the ritual. Seated on a high revolving stool in front of the glass display counter, she rested her forearm in a velvet-lined wooden stand, her hand held gracefully aloft.

The saleslady slipped each of the glove fingers on Mama's hand, massaging and gently easing them into place. Mama curled her thumb into the glove and smoothed it onto her hand. Then, using a tiny, pearl-handled buttonhook, the saleslady fastened the wrist buttons.

With each new glove, Mama held her hand up, twisting and flexing, admiring it as though it belonged to someone else. Eventually, the selection made, the gloves were reverently laid in a tissue-lined box and wrapped in elegant paper and gold cord.

The floorwalker, identified by a carnation boutonniere, nodded pleasantly to us as we walked past him, up the wide central staircase to the mezzanine. How lovely that exotic word rolled on my tongue when I tried it, after Mama repeated it for me. On the mezzanine there were comfortable plush armchairs for ladies waiting to meet shopping companions.

It also held the nursery. Mama said that in the past, when I had been too little to go shopping with her, she had left me there. I had a vague memory of white metal cribs and a nursemaid in a white cap and uniform. But now I was old enough to go along with her, and I would not have to be deserted there!

The main reason for this trip to town was to buy me a pair of shoes, and this prompted my introduction to Doerflinger's special wonderland, the children's shoe department. Mama lifted me onto a raised platform to sit in a swanboat chair, just like the ones on carousels. The salesman, as gentle as the glove saleslady, slipped off my shoes, placed my small foot in a wooden device, and holding down my nervously twitching toes, took the measurements.

After disappearing behind a curtained doorway, he returned with a stack of shoe boxes. Deftly flipping them open, he held up a shoe for Mama's inspection, then eased it onto my foot with a shoehorn, after a solemn softening of the back with the heel of his hand. One by one he tried them, buckling the straps or tying the laces quickly and firmly. I wondered if I'd *ever* learn to tie a shoe like that!

He smoothed his firm fingers over the top of the toe, pushed his thumb down to show there was sufficient growing space, then lifted me down to the floor, where I walked back and forth while they checked for "slipping at the heel."

The selection made, Mama smiled at my pleading and agreed that I could wear my new shoes. Then the salesman gave me a bright, red, gas-filled balloon.

We took the lacy black wrought-iron elevator down to the first floor. The attendant smiled at me, admired my floating balloon and my new shoes. I tried to keep up with Mama, but the shoes were stiff and the soles were slippery, and I skidded on the polished wooden floor.

Then, when I stopped to admire their shiny tops to make sure I hadn't scuffed them, Mama disappeared! Now I was abandoned, alone in the world, lost forever. I burst into loud, frantic sobs. The friendly floorwalker held my hand, and within seconds, Mama hurried to us.

"Carole Joyce!" she exclaimed. She didn't scold me, but I wondered if this meant that I would be left in the nursery in the future.

I don't know if Mama had planned it, or if the final stop of the day was to dry my tears and leave a happy memory. We walked down another flight of stairs to the Tea Shoppe, where we sat at a tiny marble-topped table and ate ice-cream sundaes from icy-cold, paper-lined silver dishes.

The excitement of the day had tired me, and on the short walk to the streetcar stop, I told Mama that my hand hurt from holding onto the balloon string. She laughed, saying she was too old to carry a balloon, and fastened it to the button on top of my tam.

Minutes later, the tam came loose from my head and sailed away, tied to the red balloon. My second tears of the afternoon turned to laughter, joining Mama's, as we watched them disappear high in the sky before we climbed onto the streetcar headed for home. ❖

-J-F-
-KERNAN-

Saturday Adventures

Chapter Three

My favorite times for outdoor adventures were Saturdays back in the Good Old Days. That probably goes without saying for most of us, since Saturday was often the time a youngster had the freedom to explore the possibilities of the great outdoors.

Saturday adventures knew no seasonal restrictions. Mother nature was always ready to share an excursion with a kid who had some time on his or her hands.

Winter weekends meant sledding on steep hills. In the country there was iceskating on thickly-frozen ponds, while our city cousins glided on rinks.

Spring and summer Saturdays were filled with fishing, family picnics, camping trips and lake parties.

But if I had to pick my favorite season for Saturday adventures, it would have to be autumn. I have an October birthday, so fall became my season. (Actually we *all* had our seasons. With birthdays in January and February, Daddy and my brother Dennis shared winter. Mama's April birthday gave her spring. Baby sister Donna, with a July birthday, nailed down the summer season for herself.)

I also looked forward to autumn because it seemed work slacked off a bit. Spring and summer Saturdays were often filled with chores centered around the growing of our food supply for the coming year.

But autumn!

So what if a cunning bunny slipped by while Blackie was leading me on a wild goose chase?

Autumn meant that squirrel or rabbit hunts wouldn't be punctuated by tick and chigger bites. The was nothing like a rousing hunt in the crisp morning air with my best friend and pet, Blackie. He wasn't much of a hunting dog, and I suppose I wasn't much of a hunter, but neither of us was all that interested in shooting something on those glorious days of fall. So what if a cunning bunny slipped by while Blackie was leading me on a wild goose—or was a wild hare—chase?

I also loved the leaves of autumn, both on the tree and off. On the tree they were like the robes of royalty, jewels shining in the woodlands around our little country home.

Off the tree the leaves might seem to be a chore. But any child who hated to rake leaves never knew the joy of jumping feetfirst or diving headlong into the pile. Blackie joined me, rollicking first and then burrowing like a groundhog. Yes, that scattered leaves in the cool autumn breeze, but boundless energy gathered them again for another round.

And then we burned them! How many frosty Saturday evenings glowed with our leafy pyres? Standing before the fire, my brother, sister and I turned like roasting rascals, warming first one side and then the other. The pungent aroma signalled a farewell to fall's beautiful foliage.

I will *never* think of autumn as the death of summer and the prelude to winter! I will remember it always as my favorite season for Saturday adventures back in the Good Old Days.

—*Ken Tate*

A Confirmed Fisherman

By Donald L. Helland

During the early 1950s, my family and I lived in a small town (population less than 100) in central North Dakota. The town had a "Tom Sawyer" atmosphere with a general store, a tiny café and a post office.

We had no organized sports and there were no movie theaters, so much of our entertainment consisted of playing football or baseball on a vacant lot, hunting rabbits and gophers, and playing cards and endless games of Monopoly in the home of one of my friends.

Our main form of entertainment in the spring and summer, however, was fishing. All winter long we looked forward to opening day of fishing season. We spent hours cleaning and oiling our reels and repainting our red-and-white and black-and-white lures.

Opening day was always May 19. It made no difference if the opener fell on a weekday or a weekend. If the opener was on a school day, my brother and I and my friend, Dale, and his brother would just skip school and go fishing. Our teachers let us get away with this because they knew how eager we were to fish. Our favorite fishing hole was a wide spot in the Sheyenne River several miles from town, at the foot of a large culvert protruding from under a gravel road.

Dale's family owned two cars. One was an old Dodge of late 1930s vintage, which they let him take hunting and fishing. We were only 14 years old and had no driver's licenses, but back then parents weren't very concerned about matters such as driver's licenses and automobile insurance.

That year, fishing season opened on a Saturday. Of course we went fishing. The fish were biting, and we were having so much fun that we decided to go fishing again the next day—Sunday. We were busy making plans until it dawned on us that Dale and I were being confirmed on Sunday at 10 a.m. at the little church in town.

Confirmation class. Author is front and center. Dale is in the back row, second from left.

After a short discussion, we all agreed that if we left early in the morning, we could fish for a while and still get back in plenty of time for the confirmation service.

At 5 a.m. Sunday morning, we headed to our fishing hole. We had a great time fishing until someone pointed out that it was 15 minutes to 10. We threw our rods into the car and raced back to town. I'm sure that was the fastest that old Dodge was ever driven.

When we got to town, we ran to our homes to wash up and change clothes.

Many heads in the congregation turned when Dale and I arrived late for the church service. Everyone knew we were being confirmed today. We marched up to the front row and joined the five other kids who were also in our confirmation class.

The pastor gave us a stern look but continued with the service, which concluded with our confirmation. He never asked why we were late, and we didn't offer any excuses.

Fifty years later, fishing is still my favorite form of recreation. I'm retired now, though, so I can fish anytime I want. I guess you can call me a confirmed fisherman. ❖

Panfish Days

By Myrtle Kenyon

I was born and raised on a farm in Friberg Township in Minnesota. The west side of our property bordered the Otter Tail River, so I had ample opportunities for swimming and bathing. In 1924 I was about 10 years old and my friend, Mildred, was 11. She lived near a good fishing lake. Her home was about a mile from my home, over the pasture and alfalfa hills. On warm summer days she would run down to my home, and we would saunter down to the river to bathe, splash water in each other's faces and make plans for a fishing expedition.

We loved to go fishing, especially in the early morning when no one else was around. On one particular Friday, we made plans to go fishing the next morning at 4 a.m. Mildred would dig the angleworms; all I'd have to do was get there on time.

Saturday morning I was there bright and early. Mildred was still fast asleep in her upstairs bedroom, so I reached up with my fish pole and tapped her bedroom window to get her attention. She got up quietly and crept downstairs and outside. We were two happy, excited girls when we got the worms and took off for the lake.

Mildred had an old wooden boat and she knew how to row, so we were on our way to our fishing spot in short order. She headed straight for the spot where the sunnies congregated. We strung the squirmy worms on our hooks and began to fish.

We could see schools of sunnies flitting about in the glassy, clear water. It proved to be no problem to catch a fish as soon as a juicy worm sank in the water above the sunnies.

In a short while we were heading for home. I had my fish in the pail I had brought for that purpose. It was half-full of unhappy sunnies covered with fresh water.

I still remember the proud, happy look on my dad's face when he saw all the fish his little girl had caught for breakfast. It didn't take him long to get those fish ready for the fry pan. And I can still picture my mom with a smile on her face, frying the fish in the big black fry pan on the old kitchen range. I had seven brothers, so it took a lot of sunnies for all of us for a meal.

I will never forget that wonderful experience. For a country kid, there couldn't be a better one. ❖

A Young Boy's Dream

By Alton E. Rinker Sr.

It's early morning, I'm down at the lake,
Just me and my fishing gear.
All my troubles and all my worries
Just seem to disappear.

I placed a worm on my fishing hook
That was tied to the end of my line.
I cast out the bait with a flick of my wrist
And watched the reel unwind.

The bait and the sinker made a big splash,
Then dropped right to the bottom.
Soon there was a tug at the end of my rod,
And I shouted, "By George, I've got him!"

He came to the top with a powerful flop,
And made a beautiful splash.
I could tell by the way he danced on his tail
That I'd hooked me a largemouth bass.

The rod was bent, the line was tense,
And I knew the fight was on.
Soon I fought him onto shore,
And he looked to be twenty inches long.

I scooped him up in my fishing net,
And was proud of the fight he had given.
As I carried him home that day in July,
I thought, *Boy, this is really livin'!*

A Special Picnic

By Mary Koeberl

Everyone loves a picnic. When I was growing up back in the 1950s, our church—like most other country churches in southeastern Missouri—held an annual community picnic.

These picnics were important social events. Each church usually scheduled its picnic so as not to conflict with the other churches. As a child, I was not aware of this; all I knew was that summertime meant picnics.

Mama and Daddy (Ruby and Joe Kranawetter) and my sisters Nancy, Kay and Carol and I spent many warm summer evenings at church picnics. Daddy had grown up in the Pocahontas, Mo., area, so we usually made it to the picnics at both churches in town—Zion Lutheran Church and St. John's Lutheran Church. Something about the picnic at St. John's Lutheran Church in Pocahontas was special. I guess I should say many things were special.

If we were lucky, Daddy would give us a whole dollar to spend. Once we arrived at the picnic, it took a long time to decide how to spend my precious money.

There were big, juicy hamburgers at the hamburger stand that smelled so good. The people who made the hamburgers worked in a little square place with screen wire all around—to keep the flies out, I guess. The people working in there always seemed to be having as much fun as the people buying the hamburgers.

I spent a great deal of time at the stand where they sold gum, candy and all kinds of neat little toys, like paper umbrellas, elaborate little fold-up fans and the infamous cap guns. The boys liked to get the cap guns and go around scaring the girls.

Ice cream was pretty high on my list of special things. You could get an extra scoop of delicious ice cream for as little as 5 or 10 cents.

I guess my favorite attraction at the picnic was the pony rides. There weren't too many other church picnics that had pony rides, and I loved to hang around and pet the ponies. Sometimes they let us bigger kids walk around with the ponies if some little kids were scared.

The entertainment was held on the flat bed of a truck or someone's hay wagon. But the acts and the music were crowd pleasers, and it was free. We didn't even mind sitting on seats made of hard oak boards resting on sawhorses.

If a child lost or spent all his money before the evening was over, he could usually make a deal with the friendly guys at the soda stand. They would give him a quarter—or a soda—if he walked around and picked up soda bottles and put them in one of their wooden cases.

There was an outdoor bowling alley where you could win stuff by knocking the pins down in so many tries. It kept some of the boys busy running back and forth setting those pins up. I usually didn't get too close to the bowling alley or hang around in that area too long because there were too many boys, and I was very shy.

A big meal of chicken and dumplings, fried chicken, ham, or kettle-cooked beef with all the trimmings—homemade bread, coffee cake and delicious pies—was also prepared for the picnic. Heavy iron kettles were set up, where the tasty beef was cooked and stirred all afternoon. Long tables were set up outside in the shaded church yard, where the girls and women served food.

Sometimes the line of people waiting to buy tickets for the supper was very long, since the church was well known for its delicious meals.

Years later, I married one of those bowling pinsetters, Leonard Koeberl, and I became a part of St. John's. Unfortunately, the church picnic as I had remembered it had been scaled down (no more pony rides or bowling alley).

Leonard and I later served on the picnic's organizing committee. Then I *really* appreciated the fun, fellowship and hard work involved. The St. John's church picnic eventually was discontinued, but it will always be one of my fondest memories from the Good Old Days. ❖

Family Picnic

By E.M. Fedenich

*D*uring the late 1920s, I was a 5-year-old girl growing up in Brooklyn, N.Y., where I shared weekend picnics with my parents and brothers, Joseph, 10, and Herbie, 4. Picnic preparations always started with Mother sending us to bed early. Sleep came reluctantly as tantalizing aromas brought mental pictures of tender, crusty chicken, deviled eggs, tangy potato salad and soft rolls baking side by side with Mother's special frosted coconut cake.

Father's share of picnic planning meant mixing salads of lettuce, tomatoes, celery and cucumbers (all fresh from our backyard garden) into waxed-paper dishes, ultimately to be placed over bags of crushed ice in our picnic hamper. Having a picnic was never complete without large dill pickles, freshly bought from a nearby delicatessen where one

My brothers were watching Father fill a cooled thermos with lemonade.

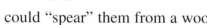

could "spear" them from a wooden barrel filled with spices and brine.

Awakening early on picnic morning, I dressed in a white sailor blouse, blue cotton knickers and a sweater, just in case it turned cool. My brothers were already at breakfast, watching Father fill a cooled thermos with freshly squeezed lemonade sweetened with tiny cherry slices and sugar.

"Everybody ready?" he'd inquire, closing the packed wicker food hamper and starting our procession out the door. Joe followed, proudly carrying the thermos, while Herbie held a folded, red-and-white checkered oilcloth that was popular as a picnic tablecloth. I held a large bag of paper goods, hoping we'd have enough napkins and such, while Mother always carried a large blanket that we sat on.

Soon we arrived at Prospect Park, where other families would have arrived early, hoping for choice grassy spots. When we selected ours, the blanket was opened and the oilcloth spread to hold the hamper contents as we listened to the municipal orchestra.

Shoo the Moos by Stevan Dohanos © 1950 SEPS: Licensed by Curtis Publishing

The musicians were smartly dressed in uniforms glistening with gold braid that shone as brightly as their instruments. They played patriotic marches and popular songs of the day, and everybody sang along.

"Can we ride the merry-go-round?" I asked. "Maybe I'll win the brass ring this time!"

"We'll all take a ride," my father agreed, "then we must start for home."

Although I didn't win many brass rings, I've never forgotten the fun of riding those painted, carved fantasy horses. I still like to ride the carousel whenever I visit amusement parks or county fairs.

Our picnic excursions changed forever when Father surprised us one evening by driving home in a big, black Ford touring automobile. It was so formidable; I had to stand on the running boards to peek through its open windows.

Father announced that we could drive to many different picnic places—so how about going out to Long Island's beautiful countryside? I had heard someone say that a princess lived in one of the new mansions that had been built to resemble castles. "Can we invite her to our picnic?" I asked. But my brothers thought looking for soldiers would be more fun.

The next morning we began our first automobile outing. The spacious backseat held all the supplies plus three excited children as Father carefully drove toward Long Island while Mother helped by reading roadside directions. Traffic in the 1920s was still moderate, but an occasional car would pass with a short horn blast and cheery "hellos" from everybody. The breeze carried hints of saltwater and sand.

"Almost there," my father often commented, driving past a turreted mansion whose endless lawns and spectacular flower gardens made me dizzy. I caught glimpses of white marble statues that seemed to watch our car as we passed. "Can we find the princess?" I asked, but Mother thought it was time to stop and eat. At that point the wicker hamper's contents took precedence over a princess.

Father brought our car to a stop next to a smooth, grassy lane, away from any traffic but not too near any of the mansions' high stone walls. No one ever asked us to leave their

1950 The General Tire & Rubber Co. ad, House of White Birches nostalgia archives

property when we picnicked; we appreciated being able to picnic on their land, and felt free to visit again. But that was in the 1920s.

Spreading our blanket under a shady tree, Mother unfolded the oilcloth. The hamper was soon emptied, satisfying five healthy appetites. My brothers often played ball—"Away from the road!" cautioned my parents—while I liked to walk on the soft grass, following a small brook that nourished bushes of wild yellow-and-white daisies. I was allowed to pick a small bunch. Then I tried to lure a monarch butterfly to land on my hand, but it gave in to shyness and flitted away, its wings catching the sun's rays in deep brown and yellow tones.

My parents were always alert to our activities, even while Father was trying to explain the Ford's mechanics to Mother, who, like many women of her generation, was eagerly learning to drive. Stretching out on the sweet-smelling grass, I would begin to feel sleepy; I'd be awakened much later by Mother's soft touch. "It's time to go home," she'd say. "I've wrapped your daisies in wet newspaper to keep them fresh."

My brothers usually finished the last of Mother's cake while I cleaned up stray crumbs and disappointed the hungry ants. Once back in our car, sitting between brothers too sleepy to argue over the best window seats, I wondered where the sun went as it made room for the moon, already faintly yellow in the sky.

I guess my only regret was that I had not met a princess.

I often wonder if today's barbecues will hold the same warm memories as yesterday's wonderful family picnics. ❖

Yesterday's Picnic

By Earl R. Bennett Sr.

Many long years ago,
when I was just a boy,
There's one thing I remember
that filled my heart with joy.
Sometimes 'twould be for supper,
after Dad got home from work,
Other times a Sunday,
when his duties he could shirk.

Mom would make a salad,
and pack us up a lunch.
In would go the Kool-Aid
and lots of things to munch.
When ere we saw the basket,
we knew what was the fare;
We'd all be so excited,
our chatter filled the air.

At last 'twould all be ready,
and we'd get in the car.
The ride seemed almost endless,
"Could it really be this far?"
Finally, though, we'd get there.
How wondrous was that place,

Dad knew it pleased Mom
by the smile that lit her face.

Perhaps near an old millhouse,
near fallen in and rotten,
Or a long-empty woods camp,
its residents long forgotten.
Perhaps on a lakeshore,
our picnic we would eat,
And let its gay ripples
lap at our feet.

She'd spread out the blanket
as we all ran about.
Simply thrilled by the difference,
we'd laugh and we'd shout.
As we gaily frolicked,
Dad would look for wood …
Fire-roasted hot dogs—
they sure tasted good.

Maybe we'd be near a field,
where wild berries were ripe.
If we kids had to pick some,

oh, how we'd gripe!
The meal was soon over,
and we kids went exploring.
Mom would keep watch
while Dad did some snoring.

Too soon shadows lengthened,
and we'd have to go home,
To bed and to dream
of the next time we'd roam.
Many years have since passed,
but the memories live on
Of the sweet happy times
those picnics did spawn.

My heart yearns so oft
for those loved ones I know,
To gather them to me,
and out on a picnic to go.
What a time we would have,
not with frolic and play,
But remembering the picnics
we shared along life's way.

This Wartime Party Was Wonderful!

By V. Frances Hill

August 1944 was a happy time for our family. My brother, Bernelle, wounded at Normandy Beach, was home on convalescent leave. One memorable weekend, numerous friends dropped by to visit, including one family who had been our neighbors before they moved from Virginia to Maryland some eight years earlier. My sister Fern and I had been classmates of their daughters, Mary and Audrey. They were staying with their relatives, the Shanks, who had a daughter, Margaret, also near our age.

We renewed our friendships and, as Mary and Audrey were leaving, they invited Fern and me to visit them that evening. So after supper, Fern and I walked out the lane to the Shank home.

As we sat on the front porch visiting, we saw Bernelle and Cousin Ted (who was helping on the farm that summer) coming out the lane. They evidently had decided to come visiting on an impulse, for Bernelle was wearing his oldest, most comfortable clothes and Ted was wearing the jeans he wore to milk the cows. When Bernelle later apologized for his clothes, Mary said warmly that he deserved to wear what he liked.

The young people gathered in the cheerful parlor for games and music. When Mary sang *The Bells of St. Mary's*, her beautiful voice thrilled me.

And Margaret was the only one who could coax much music out of her huge, old piano,

For me, there has never been another party so wonderful as that one, even though the end of the war was still a year away.

although we did prevail on Ted to play *Indian Love Call* and a few other favorites.

Later, the girls walked out to the back yard. Mrs. Shank came to the door and told us that there were hot dogs in the refrigerator, and if we brought in firewood, we could have a wiener roast. We soon had a bonfire started.

It was such a pleasant group there at that wiener roast, from Margaret's grandmother to Mary and Audrey's little sister.

As the bonfire glowed in the warm summer night, we saw two boys walking up the dark paved road in front of the house.

It turned out to be our youngest brother, Emerson, and a friend. Margaret must have been secretly delighted, for she had a crush on Emerson's friend.

At last we decided it was time to go home. It was a such beautiful moonlit night and all the young people said they would walk with us. We enjoyed a leisurely walk home—and then we laughingly suggested that we escort *them* back.

Part of the happiness of that time came from the love and security of having both parents at home, but that was to be my father's last summer. He died the following April.

Now eight from our impromptu party are no longer living.

For me, there has never been another party so wonderful as that one, even though the end of the war was still a year away.

And, whenever I remember it, I am 15 years old again. ❖

The Hayride

By Helen Colwell Oakley

In the 1930s, after the hay was gathered from the fields and tucked away in the barns for the long winters down on the farm, thoughts turned to having an old-fashioned hayride.

We lived in rural New York in those days, not far from Binghamton. Dobbin and Mollie, the beloved team of farm horses, would soon be thoroughly rested from working in the hay fields and anxious to be harnessed again. Dad had promised that there would be a hayride just as soon as all the hay was in the barn.

Mom never went on the hayride, but she was as excited as we youngsters were when hayride time came around. She baked cakes and cookies and stirred up batches of fudge for refreshments and tended to all of the other tasks of having an old-fashioned hayride down on the farm.

The party line would be busy ringing all day long as time for the hayride drew near. Sometimes there would be several neighbors on the line at once discussing the hayride. Party lines were often a nuisance when discussing a confidential matter, but they were helpful and enjoyable at other times.

Chores were completed in record-breaking time on the evening of a hayride, with the cows all turned out to pasture while it was still twilight. The horses neighed and whinnied loudly as if to say, "Turn us out to pasture, too!" Their time would come later when they would be harnessed to the hay riggin' by the hired man. Tiny bells were attached to their harness for special occasions. How enchanting and melodious they were, jingling through the night as we made our way slowly over the country lanes.

The hay riggin' was packed all over with layers of soft, new hay, so fragrantly fresh.

We all piled up onto the wagon, then snuggled down into the hay for the exciting ride beneath millions of twinkling stars and an enormously full, golden moon. Someone was sure to bring a banjo or ukulele to accompany the joyful blending of voices ringing out in the quietness of the summery country evening.

The singing and riding were fun, but I remember best the moments of sheer beauty when quiet set in in the woodlands as we glided along underneath the great white way as if on a magical sea. Our hayrides were romantic and enchanting.

Someone was sure to bring a ukulele to accompany the joyful voices.

Mom and the other ladies must have been on the lookout for the hayride party to return, for bonfires and the fireplace were smoking and ready for roasting hot dogs and grilling hamburgers. There must have been hundreds of hot dogs and dozens of hamburgers to feed us.

The picnic table held the supplies and the guests nestled down on the warm ground with their plates heaped full. Most everyone wanted to roast his own hot dog on a long stick over the coals of the bonfire. Along with the hot dogs and hamburgers there were salads, baked beans, relishes, rolls, fruit punch and a variety of cakes and desserts. Everything tasted so delicious, eating out in the open and all together. Later on there would be a freezer of homemade custard ice cream and toasting marshmallows over the dying embers.

The fragrances of new-mown hay, bonfires and smoking fireplaces have a tendency to revive the pleasure and enchantment of those good old-fashioned hayrides down on the farm. And the teams of horses gently pulling the hay riggings over the country lanes were memorable. The thought of it fills my heart with nostalgia for the beauty of the Good Old Days. ❖

The Roller Rink

By Rita Bonini Long

Growing up in Ridgway, Pa., during the 1950s, part of our daily fun was putting on roller skates and working to perfect our skills on the way to becoming the best skaters in the neighborhood. Just about every kid had a pair of skates, the kind that clamped onto shoes and were kept on by the skillful turn of the skate key, which one was never without. I spent many a happy day skating up and down the streets, flying off curbs and doing midair turns. My maneuvers sometimes led to parts of my anatomy meeting the sidewalk "up close and personal," and generally kept my mother busy running for the iodine and Band-Aids.

I know that there were times when she would have preferred that her daughter pursue more feminine activities, but growing up in a neighborhood full of boys with only two other girls my age to play with, I had to learn to hold my own. I was never very athletically inclined—I was always the last chosen in games—but skating was something I was good at.

Someone was going to build a skating rink on Boot Jack Hill!

One day exciting news spread through the town: Someone was going to build a skating rink on Boot Jack Hill! This was great news for kids of all ages. Since the rink would be enclosed in a building, we would not have to stop skating during the winter months.

Ridgway, located in the mountains of northern Pennsylvania, was known for very heavy winter snows, and most people went ice-skating, but that did not really appeal to me.

We waited with great anticipation for the construction to begin, and then waited impatiently for it to end. In time, our waiting was over and the day for the grand opening arrived. Everyone was there; we couldn't wait to get inside. We were not disappointed!

The rink was in a large building that also contained a small restaurant where we could buy all the necessary staples of teenage life—you know, hamburgers, hot dogs, fries and soda.

There was also an area where we could rent boot skates that came up to midcalf. Boys wore black skates and girls wore white. My dear mom thrilled me when she bought me a pair for Christmas that year.

The rink was circular, and partially surrounded by railings where people who were still trying to get the hang of it would hang on for dear life to avoid getting run over by the "experts." The rest of the rink was bounded by walls, with double doors every few feet.

In these pre–air conditioning days, the doors were left open during the summer to improve air circulation. Music was constantly piped in, and some people worked out dance routines that were really spectacular.

Hanging from the middle of the ceiling was a mirrored ball that spun around. Sometimes the regular lighting was turned off and the spotlights were turned on. As the ball spun, the effect was that of a thousand shimmering diamonds. It was absolutely breathtaking.

An interesting—if not dangerous—part of skating at the rink was a game called The Whip. One skater would grab hold of another person's hand and the second person would do the same.

This would continue until a long line of people were skating together at high speed, screaming and laughing their heads off.

Being a teen and very fearless (or stupid, as we all tend to be at that age), I was willing to try anything. So, as the line passed me, my friend grabbed my hand and we joined the whip. I did this many times and enjoyed it. However, one night I ended up being the last person on the chain. This was not a very good place to be, as I was to soon find out.

The leaders of the chain went faster and faster, and the person who was holding on to me began to get a sweaty palm. I felt my hand slipping out of hers just as we approached the open double doors. You guessed it. I became airborne briefly, until the gravel parking lot met me on my way down. I lay there with the wind knocked out of me until everyone determined that I was not dead.

Then I was taken to the hospital emergency room. I had been wearing shorts and a short-sleeved blouse, and they had to pick the gravel out of my legs and arms.

My poor mother was called to the hospital. After regaining her composure, she felt that my skates should be banished to the attic for 20 years or so to assure that I would actually make it to adulthood in one piece.

In time, I persuaded her that I would try to be more careful. I enjoyed several more years of fun at the rink. Many times after my "maiden flight," I took part in other formations of the whip. But I was smarter now; never again was I the last one on the chain—much to my mother's relief! ❖

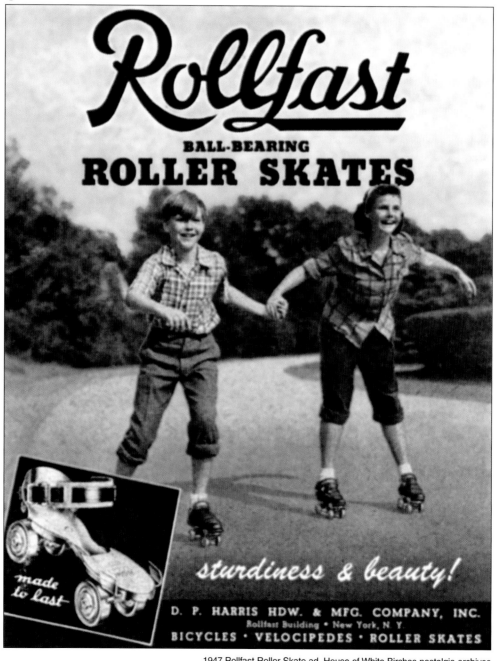

1947 Rollfast Roller Skate ad, House of White Birches nostalgia archives

Roller Magic

By Ann Oliver

I recently attended a birthday party for my grandson that was held at the new skating complex in our city. You don't say "skating rink" anymore. It is "rollerplex" or something else. There was a restaurant inside, flashing lights led to a game area, and at one end was a giant screen showing sports events.

But the thing that amazed me was the quiet. With most everyone skating on the new roller-blade-type skates, there was no clatter of steel rollers on wooden floors.

My mind went back to another time, the 1940s in Tyler, Texas, when skating rinks were quite different. When I was a young child, we did all our skating on sidewalks, wearing our skate key around our neck or in a pocket. We would skate all over town, and we especially delighted in finding an abandoned filling station or a slab where a building had once stood. There we could hone our skills, turning and skating in circles on the vast expanse of concrete.

When I reached junior high and high school, there was a rink on the outskirts of town by a lake with picnic tables. Since most people had no cars, it was used mostly for church and school events. Once a group of us decided to hike out to it, but we were so tired when we got there that it was difficult to skate.

As I reached adulthood, there was a rink inside the city limits that quickly became the hangout for young adults on Friday nights. We skated the night away to the organ strains of *You Can't Be True, Dear.*

Many a romance had its start in that place. In fact, I had met my current boyfriend there. He was the Fred Astaire of the skating rink. Tall and agile, he could swirl and dip and dance on those skates like nothing I had seen before. I was just a mediocre skater myself, so I loved it when they had couples-only skating. Then I became Ginger Rogers to his Fred Astaire, for in the confines of his strong arms, I could swirl and dip and do all the things I could never do alone. It was my favorite time of the evening!

The rink had no fancy snack bar—just a soft-drink machine and benches against a wall. The loud music and the din of skates made

conversation almost impossible. So we stayed on the floor and skated until it was time to go.

Afterward we would all pile into a few cars and head for the drive-in for frosty mugs of root beer. There we all parked close together and had the conversations we could not have at the rink. When we finally headed off in different directions, we would yell, "See you next Friday!"

That's the way skating was back in the Good Old Days. I wouldn't trade those memories for all the glitz of modern rollerplexes. ❖

JOHN FALTER

Skating Parties

By Douglas B. Cameron

When I was growing up in a small New England village during the 1950s, the activity many of us looked forward to most was ice-skating. My cousins and I lived next-door to each other, and we were fortunate to have a skating "rink" practically in our back yard. It wasn't the typical commercial-type skating rink that we think of today. It was actually an old cranberry bog that had to be cleared of its overgrowth each fall.

Each year, our families met on a weekend—usually in late October—to begin clearing away the year's accumulation of vegetation. We gathered all the brush in the center of the clearing and built a large bonfire. Once the overgrowth had been consumed and the remnants of the fire cleared, we dammed up the slow-moving feeder brook at the exit point of the bog with heavy planks.

Over the next few days, the brook gradually flooded the bog, creating a shallow pond. After years of trial and error, we learned to gauge the depth we wanted so that it back-flooded into the woods, forming channels on what had been footpaths.

We were not allowed on the ice until one of our parents declared it safe.

The first hard freeze usually arrived a couple of weeks after Thanksgiving. However, we were not allowed on the ice until one of our parents declared it safe, even though the water was only 2 or 3 feet deep at its deepest point.

When the ice was solid enough, we strung lights around the perimeter of the rink and into the channels to permit nighttime skating. There was a small summer cottage next to the rink where we could change into our skates and get out of the cold. We covered the hardwood floors with panels of dense wallboard so that our skates would not scratch them. When it was bitterly cold—as it often can be in that region—we built a fire in the fireplace to warm us.

As soon as we got home from school, we wasted no time in changing into warm clothing and heading to the skating rink. The first couple of times on skates, our ankles were so weak and wobbly that we could hardly stand. But they soon strengthened. Frequently, my cousins and I had to be summoned home for supper and homework well after sunset, never mind how cold it was outside.

The skating-party idea originated with our parents. They had hosted one for several years. A few days before the party, my dad—a volunteer fireman—would obtain several lengths of hose from the fire station and run it to a hydrant several hundred yards away. He flooded the rink with an inch or so of water to recondition its surface. Then we hoped for a

windless night so that the surface would freeze to a smooth, glassy finish. From that day until the party, no one was allowed on the ice.

This party was one of the social highlights of the season for our parents' friends. Most who attended actually tried their skates, though for many, it was the only time during the season that they wore them. The lights created an almost surreal scene as couples glided arm-in-arm over the ice to the sounds of Strauss waltzes and other tunes coming from large high-fidelity speakers.

The skill levels of these folks ranged across the board; a few were accomplished figure skaters, but quite a few more seemed to have no business being on skates. Though our parents would have disapproved, my cousins and I snuck into the woods after the party was well underway and watched the skaters. It frequently took a lot of self-control to not give ourselves away, especially when we watched someone fall on his backside, skates and arms flailing. Fortunately, no one ever suffered a serious injury.

When the skaters got too cold or tired, they retired to a cocktail and dinner party hosted at my aunt and uncle's nearby home, a large summer inn. About 75 of their friends attended, and everyone had a wonderful, memorable time.

When I was in grammar school, I asked my parents to hold a similar event so my cousins and I could invite our friends. Of course, the cocktails and sit-down dinner were replaced with sodas, hot dogs and chips. We issued a general invitation to our classmates, and on the appointed afternoon during a weekend in January or February, everyone arrived and immediately took to the ice. Soon the rink was alive with 30 or 40 rambunctious youngsters.

My dad, a powerful skater in his own right, towed around a dozen or so of us as we hung on to each other's waists to perform the ever-popular "whip." A firm grip was essential to withstand the force generated when we "cracked the whip." Those at the very end inevitably let go, careening off into a snowbank or underbrush.

Many of our friends were good skaters, and we held races around the outer edge of the rink and through the channels. It's a wonder none of us ever impaled himself on a sharp branch or smashed into one of the many boulders around the edge of the pond.

One year, a buddy coerced me into turning the lights out for a few seconds so he could sneak a kiss from a girl he liked. After he positioned himself strategically, I pulled the plug. All the girls screamed—and I caught heck from my mother when she found out why I'd done it.

Once we reached high school, our interests changed. Skating parties became a thing of the past as sports, dating, dances and ski trips dominated our free time. But I still enjoyed skating, and I frequented our rink to practice my hockey skills or just enjoy the pleasure of gliding over the ice.

Our skating rink eventually was dredged out into a smaller but deeper pond that my uncle used to irrigate his inn's extensive grounds. Little remains of the old rink now; but the memories of the fun we all had—especially the skating parties—will live on forever. ❖

The WPA Rink

By Audrey Carli

The Great Depression, with its hard times and lean years, is still spoken of in dreary tones. But there was a magical element in the 1940s that provided the citizens in our northern Michigan community in Gogebic County with winter fun that many of us still recall with nostalgia! The fun came from ice-skating in the stone building with the rounded roof on the edge of Sunday Lake. It had been built by Works Progress Administration (WPA) workers who were paid by the federal government.

Because of the Depression, those men would have been unemployed otherwise. We wondered if the government people ever dreamed that the project would provide such happy results, as well as jobs!

When the wailing north wind blew in December, chilling us and making the utility wires hum, it was time for children, teens and adults to fetch their skates and walk or ride to the WPA rink to glide around to peppy music.

It was time for everyone to fetch their skates and go to the WPA rink.

No matter that snowplows had to drive around to keep the roads clear, or that the snowbanks looked like fluffy icing; the ice rink promised exercise, companionship and fun.

Many of us skaters from that era recall pushing open the heavy door and hearing the burst of music blaring from the speakers. We hurried to the side rooms (one for boys and one for girls) and laced up our skates. Then we hobbled on our blades to the door, pushed it open and glided out onto the glassy ice.

Music pulsed as we launched into the evening with dramatic glides and delight! Our sharp blades cut crisply under our feet. The cold, invigorating air chilled our nostrils as we skated around and around.

The talented figure skaters stayed in the center to do their twirls and figure eights. One talented lady, Mrs. Laird, reminded us of the figure skaters we saw in movies; we enjoyed watching her glide and twirl gracefully in time to the soothing melodies.

As an "ordinary skater" in the days of my childhood and teen years, I skated on the outer edge of the oval rink, enjoying the beat of popular songs. But there were also classical melodies, such as Strauss waltzes, and other tunes that made skaters' legs move in rhythm.

Of course there was boy-girl socializing as well. "Want to skate?" a boy would ask a girl. Usually she smiled and nodded and the pair joined hands as they skated around in time to the music. The cold air seemed to tingle with merriment!

As a boy and girl skated together, they talked about school, neighborhood topics, future plans or just plain nonsense. Then, when the song ended, the pair split, with him calling out, "Thanks for skating!" And the next boy glided up on silvery runners to ask to skate.

It continued that way all evening until intermission, when the music paused for the announcement that the rink should be cleared so the cleanup crew could sweep off the ice. We all went into the bleachers around the rink and watched as teenage boys with wide, wicked-looking brooms skated back and forth, pushing heaps of flaked-off ice that resembled mushy snow. After a few minutes the ice was again crystal clear, except for some almost invisible cut marks from the numerous blades engraving the evening's history.

When intermission ended, the crowd rushed back onto the ice and the music and fun picked up right where it had left off.

Soon the caretaker, Mr. Forte, came to warn us to start taking off our skates. "Time to close!"

We babbled in the changing room again in the din of laughter and conversation. Sometimes there were special plans to punctuate the evening. Oftentimes a boy would ask a girl if he could walk her home. Then they hardly noticed the blustery winter wind blowing loose snow across the road.

Questions galore passed between the pair, and talk about the next skating session melted into fresh plans to skate.

The next day in school, clusters of us girls would be chattering about the previous night's fun.

It might seem like we skated anytime we felt like it. But there were those also times when a friend responded to a routine skating invitation with "I can't go skating; too much schoolwork."

Nevertheless, no matter what, teenagers gathered several times a week at the WPA indoor ice rink. It was a brightly lit place where we were entertained as we socialized, even while the wind howled and snow blew in white mists outside under the dark winter sky.

Even today, as memories linger, shrieks of teenage laughter still ring in my mind. Then I long for the happy times when our pleasures were wholesome.

Life was not affluent, but it was more carefree and less complicated, thanks in part to the WPA ice rink! ❖

Woman Skater by Guy Hoff © 1933 SEPS: Licensed by Curtis Publishing

Days at the Rink

By D.A. Guiliani

y first trip to the ice rink was at age 4, when I tagged along with my 8-year-old sister and her friends. The ice rink became life for me and my friends from that beginning in 1946 until I hit high school, when school activities took over. But those skating years were special. Brisk winds came down from Canada, chilling the air even more as they crossed Lake Superior, the deepest and coldest of the Great Lakes. We kids on the East Side of Iron Mountain, Mich., knew those winds meant one thing: The rink would be flooded. Adults might grumble about shoveling the fresh snow almost daily, but we scurried to the highboy in our room to dig out the wool socks that Grandma had knitted for us. One pair of those socks and your feet were warm in the skate boot.

Life in winter was lived on the rink. The price was right—free! The city took care of the ice. After a few nights of plunging temperatures from the far north, the men from the city crew plied their skills.

The initial layer of water was pumped through wide hoses, covering the baseball field just off East "A" Street. After the first ice layer was 4–5 inches thick, a street department truck filled with water drove to the center of the rink and moved around it on a circular path. The back end of the truck had a broad, 3-inch metal pipe with tiny holes that cast an even, fine spray on the ice. From the road entering the rink area, you'd swear the rink wore a glass covering. Twice each week, this thin, soft layer was added, giving us a smooth finish throughout the entire season.

In this case, "adult" meant age 14 and older—not X-rated.

In our town of 9,000, the West Side had a rink, too, but no warming house. The North Side had a rink and warming house, but not a volunteer association. We East Siders had all three, so our rink was the place to be.

In summer, the men who volunteered to keep the rink going canvassed the East Side door-to-door, seeking donations. Most folks gave a buck or two. This money purchased hand soap and toilet paper for the warming-house bathrooms, brooms and snow shovels for keeping the floor of the log warming house and canvas-covered walkway to the ice clean and clear, and treats for Sunday-night adult skating parties. In this case, "adult" meant age 14 and older, not X-rated.

These volunteers also kept a fire going in the woodstove, the building clean, records playing over the PA system and the concession stand open. The men had the implied authority to eject any problem-causers. In other words, no fighting was tolerated. The names Salmeen, Mongrain, Larson, Peterson, Eiseman and Johnson were heard again and again in the volunteer roll call.

On school nights the rink was open 6:30–9 p.m. This was a great motivator to hurry home to do schoolwork so you could leave right after the supper dishes had been washed and dried.

On weekends the rink was open in the afternoon and evening. During the afternoons, Mr. and Mrs. Carl Eiseman were there. He helped with chores; she gave free lessons. A rumor floated around town that she had been a professional skater on the East Coast. Watching her, it was easy to believe that rumor. She taught us spins and jumps and fancy steps. Once you learned the basic figure, she'd move your arm to the correct position, show you how to hold your back in an artistic pose, and teach you how to complete a move to refine the figure.

The Eisemans, Toivo Salmeens, Ed Mongrains and others organized annual ice shows. A queen was crowned, and she stood on an ice-block throne that had blue lights behind it. What a breathtaking scene!

These shows had large-group acts as well as solos. The Kazda twins, Judy and Jan, from nearby Aurora, Wis., sparkled in their mirrored spins and jumps. Our own Upper Peninsula singles skating champion, Bonnie Larson, was a blond beauty, graceful and athletic. She could hold a butterfly for a full turn around the rink. Louis Pellegrini, a man from Norway, Mich., nine miles from Iron Mountain, did his clown act, tripping and slipping but never falling, which required enormous blade control. The organizing couples danced a waltz, the men in their suits and the women in sparkling gowns.

The best of Sunday afternoons had 500–600 skaters, all moving in one direction. There were no "steal the flag" games, no practicing jumps or spins. We all skated to Strauss waltzes or singles by contemporary artists such as Patti Page, Perry Como and Nat King Cole.

Sunday nights were restricted to adults, meaning high-school freshmen and older. We skated with partners just as if we were at a dance. At 8:30, a grand march was directed over the PA system. Afterward, free hot chocolate and Danish rolls were served in the warming house.

Today, open skating at the ice arena is held early in the mornings before hockey practice, and there's an admission fee.

The ball field lies dormant and white, but as I drive by, I remember those 1940s and 1950s, and from time to time I can almost hear *Don't Let the Stars Get in Your Eyes* and *Tales from the Vienna Woods*.

I wonder if these old ankles could manage a spin around the ice. I think I'll just enjoy the warm memories. ❖

1933 *Woman's World* magazine, House of White Birches nostalgia archives

The Daredevils of Dead Man's Hill

By Robert J. Miller

Because of the tough times, my parents sent me to live with my grandmother in the summer of 1934 with the expectation that I'd stay for the coming school year. Grandma lived in Johnsonburg, a small mill town in the Allegheny Mountains of northwestern Pennsylvania. She had a large house astride the borough's border in a section aptly named Clarion Heights. Beyond the town's limits, she had a couple of acres of hillside farmland. Hers was the last house on a road that climbed into the woods that surrounded town. From her front yard, one could see almost the entire town, and could look down upon the B&O station, the creek in the valley below, and the state highway on the opposite hillside.

Shortly after my arrival, Grandma introduced me to the family next door. They had three children about my age, Larry, Dorothy and Mary.

As he flashed by me, I thought I saw a look of fright on his face.

We became fast friends as we played together. Even though I was a dumb city kid and a year and a half younger than he was, Larry let me tag along when he and his chums roamed the area looking for things to do.

They kindly showed me their haunts and hideaways. Each place had a descriptive name, like Duck Rock, Picnic Rock, Airplane Tree, Grassy Road and The Flat. For a city kid in the country, that summer was full of new friends, adventure and fun!

I was fascinated by a place they called Dead Man's Hill. This short, very steep street connected Grandma's street with a road leading back into the hills. The roadway spilled onto a level spot at the intersection alongside the B&O station, crossed the railroad tracks, entered a downhill S-curve leading to the bridge over Clarion Creek, and continued straight over the valley floor for about a quarter of a mile to the center of town. It was named Dead Man's Hill because it had been the scene of numerous accidents when motorists lost control of their vehicles while descending it.

As I had expected, I was enrolled in the local school as a fourth-grade student. The new school was both frustrating and interesting. I had some difficulty adjusting to the teaching methods, which seemed strange as compared to my old school. Nonetheless, it was fun to walk down the hill, across the valley and up another hill with my new friends every day.

The winter of 1935 was extremely harsh. It was always cold, and it seemed to snow every two or three days. Since the school did not observe "snow days," it was sometimes hard to get to class on time.

However, after school and on Saturdays, the fun began. All the kids in the neighborhood brought out their sleds and coasted down the hilly streets until they were summoned home.

Larry had a Flexible Flyer. He let me use it a few times, but he wouldn't let me ride it down Dead Man's Hill.

After every snowfall, Larry and his buddies held sled races down the slope there. From a standing start they'd slide down the steep roadway, through the intersection at the bottom, over the B&O tracks, into the S-curve and across the bridge to the straightaway toward town. Sometimes they'd have speed races; other times they'd go for distance.

Even though I was the new kid in town and didn't have a sled, they let me participate. Often Larry handed me a red cloth tied to a stick and told me to act as the "starter." I had to stand at the bottom of the hill and watch for oncoming traffic, both auto and train. If I saw a train or a car approaching, I'd wave the red flag. When all was clear, I'd take off my cap and motion for the race to begin.

Although I didn't actually get to ride in a race, it was thrilling to watch the participants

speed by, bouncing over the railroad tracks and down onto the bridge. Sometimes a contestant lost control of his sled and crashed into a snowbank. Fortunately, no one ever was seriously hurt.

That winter, Larry somehow acquired a pair of skis. Lacking an instructor, he had to learn to ski on his own by making short runs down the hilly street. After awhile he became skilled enough to extend the runs.

One day he asked me to go with him to Dead Man's Hill and act as his lookout. As we trudged through a fresh snowfall, he told me that many of his friends had dared him to ski down that slope. He had accepted their challenge. I watched fearfully as he climbed to the top of the hill, strapped on the skis, and waited for my all-clear signal. When I waved my cap, he pushed off to the cheers of the onlookers, and within seconds, Larry was speeding toward the intersection.

As he flashed by me I thought I saw a look of fright on his face. Nonetheless, he continued speeding through the intersection and over the tracks. Then, as he crossed the tracks, he went airborne due to the dip in the road. He flew right over the S-curve and made an awkward landing near the bridge. His momentum carried him over the guardrail and into a snowbank.

We all rushed to the site and dug him out with our bare hands. Larry was visibly shaken, and his face was as pale as the snow that covered him. He was alright, except for a few bruises. But one of his skis had caught the edge of the guardrail and had snapped in half.

Although he was shaken, Larry was glad when he realized that he had won the dare. We all agreed that he had become the ultimate daredevil of Dead Man's Hill ❖

King of the Hill

By Joseph A. Kistner

As I remember it, it was winter in 1931 and I was 10 years old. My oldest sister took me downtown in Poughkeepsie, N.Y., and bought me, no ordinary sled, but a Flexible Flyer Racer.

Now, for a 10-year-old boy, this was a dream come true. The Flexible Flyer Racer was different from any of the other sleds the kids on the hill had. It was built long and low to the ground, and the runners were made so they would bend to the right or left, according to which direction I wanted to steer. The runners also were grooved to keep it from sliding when rounding corners.

My Flexible Flyer Racer was the focus of awe and envy the first time I brought it over to our sledding hill. After all, it was during the Great Depression, and money was more apt to be spent on food than sleds.

But my sister had a job as a stenographer for the Hornbeck Reo automobile dealership. She earned $15 each week, and she had saved a little each week to buy the sled for me.

Our hill was unusual in that it was steep for only a short distance. On it, we created a track that went into a curve leading to a gently sloping cow path about a quarter-mile long. To make sure that the track would give us a fast start, we poured water on it during freezing weather.

We held contests to see whose sled went farthest. The trick to a long ride was to run a short distance at the top of the hill and then plop down on the sled for the ride. I had a big advantage at the curve. The others had to drag their feet to stay on track, but I could steer my Flexible Flyer around the curve while losing very little speed. My sled did so well that my rivals were soon calling me "The King of the Hill."

I had a great time with my Racer until I was a teenager and other activities took over. After that, it didn't get much use until I married and our children came along. When they grew up, it was a few years before some of our grandchildren took over.

The latest were 11-year-old Sara and 8-year-old Matt. They are used to riding plastic toboggans and snow tubes, but during a recent visit, they tried out the old Racer. They had a good time riding on the sled that, more than 70 years ago, was The King of the Hill. ❖

Memories of Winter

By Larry Mahar

This is the hill where the boyish thrill
Of sledding 'neath the snow-capped fir
Held us fast 'gainst the wintry blast
And kept us all astir.
This is the hill whose biting cold
Drove us to the coffee urn,
And, pausing there,
We'd thirst for cold
And wish we could return.
This is the hill where yet I thrill
As memories unfold.
But it's getting late and I must go.
My feet are getting cold.

Weekend Fun

By LaVonne M. Sparkman

After World War II ended in 1945, we returned to our old home of Bremerton, Wash., where my parents had worked at the Naval Ammunition Depot. Sugar was still rationed when my mother decided to entertain my Sunday school class of teenagers with a doughnut party one Saturday night. Each person was to furnish a cup of sugar for the batter.

Eagerly we awaited the first batch of the sweet treat, but the first bite nearly choked us. All we could taste was salt. When my mother checked the containers of sugar, she found that the one she had used was mostly salt. She thought it was probably someone's idea of a joke, but she was angry about the waste. Later we found out what had happened. There were sisters whose brother had been camping. When he returned, his mother dumped a jar of what she thought was sugar into her sugar bin, but it was salt. Mystery solved; anger cooled.

Another time my mother hosted a taffy pull. First a syrup was cooked to hard-ball stage, then allowed to cool until barely warm.

Each of us gathered up a blob with buttered hands and began pulling.

Each of us gathered up a blob of the mixture with buttered hands and began pulling. As we stretched it and looped it together, the clear confection began to turn white and acquired the desired texture. We spread thin strips on waxed paper; when it reached room temperature, it was ready to eat.

A dozen or more teenagers enjoyed the fun and the resulting candy, but for days afterward we found sticky bits of taffy in surprising places all around the house, even under sofa cushions.

Our group included young people in our small hometown who attended the only church there. We had about 15 teens. One fellow was a little older than most of us, and he led many of our activities. He had the only car, a Model A, complete with rumble seat. Was he popular? Indeed! But he never showed any partiality to any of us girls.

Our one-room church didn't have electricity. Evening services and revivals were held under the bluish light of gas lights. They were mounted on pulleys so they could be lowered for igniting and refilling. I can still hear their soft sputter. Wires strung across the room held bedsheet curtains to divide off "rooms" for the Sunday school classes to meet separately. Teachers had to compete with the hubbub of the other classes, but that didn't keep us from learning our Bible stories.

In summer, our group frequently had our own Sunday evening vesper services around a campfire. Although most of our activities were for enjoyment, we took these services seriously.

We sponsored weekend holiday parties for the community's kids. We were allowed to use the empty school building, which we decorated elaborately. For Halloween, we constructed a "house of horrors" in one room that pleasantly scared smaller children. We directed games and contests, and we furnished refreshments.

One year we performed an old-fashioned melodrama complete with an innocent young heroine in danger of being evicted from her home by the villain. Confetti thrown through the door served as blowing snow as the hero burst in, declaring, "It ain't a fit night out fer man nor beast!"

Summer Saturday afternoons meant swimming parties. Many of those were held in Mill Creek, which crossed our property. A nice swimming hole had

Taffy Pull by Charles Berger, House of White Birches nostalgia archives

formed in a bend. A big log slanted from the high bank into the deepest part, making a handy ladder to walk down or dive from.

A roller-skating party in the nearest city was a big event for us teenagers. We all knew how to skate; we had learned on old metal skates that clamped onto our shoe soles and were held across the instep with leather straps. Lacking sidewalks, we were lucky to have learned to skate in the old, original schoolhouse, which was empty. We merrily skated many miles around and around in the dust, our chatter and laughter accompanied by the loud rumble of metal wheels.

Our youth group had a memorable experience once on Easter Sunday. By getting up very early and driving to the summit of Chinook Pass, we saw the sunrise on Mt. Rainier and had a worship service.

A very important event in my life, as for all teenagers, was learning to drive. In the '40s, there were no learner permits. When I was almost 16, my father was going to teach me how

to drive our Chevy. He was nervous, which certainly didn't contribute to my confidence.

During one of my first lessons, I was starting downhill when I was closer to the edge than my dad thought I should be and he grabbed the steering wheel. That threw me into a near-panic and scared me out of driving.

More than a year later, I was ready to try again. I asked permission to take the car out by myself to practice on a little traveled road.

Soon I accomplished shifting gears without grinding them and learned to parallel park. I was 17 years old before I felt ready to face the formidable driving test. The written part was easy, and I did pass the driving part.

One of the few times I drove to school, my mother told me to get gasoline before starting for home. But I had a couple of girls as passengers, and in the excitement and pride of being able to drive, I forgot about it. When we were almost home, the car sputtered to a stop on the main highway. How embarrassing!

I had one accident. As I turned off into our yard, suddenly the car had no brakes. I was going slowly, but couldn't stop. The car eased into a big pile of stove wood, tipping it over and stopping the car. There was no damage to the car or to my reputation.

I rode the school bus to high school 10 miles each way. The typical bus of those days had a row of seats down the middle and bench seats along each side. Everyone had to squeeze by all those legs and feet when getting on and off. Frequently toes were stepped on.

When I was a high school student, the weekdays from Monday to Friday seemed like a long time indeed as I awaited our weekend fun. Now, as a senior citizen, I am amazed at how the weeks seem to whiz by!

Of course, those years weren't all fun. But I don't want to forget those Good Old Days when I was a teenager, back in the '40s. ❖

Saturday Night Revelry

Chapter Four

When we think back to the days of our courtship, my dear wife, Janice, and I can't help but wonder if fate or Providence brought us together on that Saturday night all those decades ago.

Janice and I grew up a stone's throw apart, but separated by three years and a thin demarcation called the Missouri-Arkansas state line.

She was 17 and still in high school in a small Arkansas town.

I was 20, already out of my rural Missouri school and in my third year of college. That Saturday night she was working at a little diner, and I was looking for somewhere to have a late-night cup of coffee after a college Valentine's dance.

She waited on me, and we began to talk about the dance and the music the band had played. She loved to dance and loved music. I did, too.

I also liked talking to this vivacious redhead, so my cup of coffee turned into a meal and another hour of conversation, at least when she wasn't taking care of her other customers.

That began a predictable routine. Every Saturday night for nearly four months I was on a counter stool or in one of the diner's booths, praying that she would be my waitress.

It took me that long to work up the courage to ask her out. She had just graduated high school when she agreed to go out with me on the first Saturday night of June (with her father's permission, of course).

From then on, her Saturday nights and mine were always spent together. Whether it was a movie, bowling, informal dances at a friend's home or, yes, even at her workplace, we were inseperable.

One year later, on the anniversary of that first date, we exchanged rings and vows. She's been my "steady" ever since.

> *From then on, her Saturday nights and mine were always spent together.*

Dancing and music continued to be an important part of our lives. As many Saturday nights as possible, we found ourselves at ball rooms, square dances and music parties. We learned new steps. We even taught dance classes a few times.

Those Saturday nights became a little tougher to manage after our children got older. Parenting took precedence, but we knew we would get back to our Saturday night dates as soon as we could.

Poignantly, we watched as our teenage son met his own vivacious redhead at church, and the cycle of Saturday nights began anew. Four years later, also on the anniversary of their first date, they exchanged rings and vows, just like Mama and Papa.

Janice and I still enjoy Saturday nights out. Both of us still enjoy listening to good music and dancing. My doctor tells me its good for my heart. I tell him it must be.

After all, it was dancing, music and Saturday night revelry that led my heart to the love of my life back in the Good Old Days.

—*Ken Tate*

Jukebox Dance Parties

By Donna McGuire Tanner

I was 11 years old in 1958 when suddenly I found myself drawn to our Admiral black-and-white television set on Saturday afternoons. *Howdy Doody* had taken a backseat to *Jukebox Dance Party* on our local station WOAY in Oak Hill, W.Va.

Every Saturday, students at different high schools were invited to the television studio to dance to the latest rock-and-roll music. It was fashioned after the nationwide program *American Bandstand*. Not only was there live dancing, but local bands also performed. My uncle Philip Workman, who performed on radio, was sometimes asked to perform on the *Dance Party*.

The age limit on the program was 13 years old, and I wished I could be on the program. Then it happened.

One evening I was walking up the hill to my house from our bus stop with my older neighbor friend, Jean Craddock. She was already a student at Pax High School. I gasped when she told me that the school was going to be on my favorite program that very Saturday. How lucky she was to be going!

Then it happened. Jean told me that she had an extra ticket, and she asked if I would like to go. *Would I!*

But then my bubble burst. First problem—I was not 13. But my friend said I could pass if I pulled my long, blond hair into a ponytail, and she had the perfect dress that she would give me. Maybe it would work.

But I had another hurdle, and this was a *big problem*—my very strict parents, Basil and Rachel. However, after a lot of begging, and Jean and her mother talking on my behalf, my parents finally caved in to my whining. After all, they could watch me on television.

That Saturday when my father pulled his car up in front of the TV station, he told me he would be there to pick me up right after the program. Then he raced the 15 miles home to watch the program.

I can still feel the electric buzz going through the crowd of teens as we waited for the theme music. I thought I was going to faint when the red light of the big camera flashed on. When I saw my image on the monitor, my young world changed forever.

During the rest break midway through the program, there was a team quiz contest. Each week, students from the school appearing on the program that day competed against the reigning champs. We were so proud when the Pax team won that week. They held on to the championship for many months.

Before I knew it, it was over. As I was walking toward the door, the host of the program, Shirley Love, stopped me. Shirley was the host of most of the programs on WOAY. He invited me to come back any Saturday that I wanted. I thanked him and danced all the way to my dad's car.

That day began a tradition for Dad and me. Across from the station was a drive-in restaurant called the Top Hat. Dad pulled over there and ordered us both a glass of Coca-Cola. Time alone with either of my parents was a treasure.

On Saturday afternoons well into the early 1960s, if anyone wanted to find me, all they had to do was turn on the television set. Those were Saturdays to remember! ❖

Facing page and above: *Different Dancing Styles* by Thornton Utz © 1961 SEPS: Licensed by Curtis Publishing

Your Hit Parade

By Jan Holden

*Y*our Hit Parade was the first adult television program I remember. Like most kids growing up in the 1950s, I was glued to the set on Saturday mornings. Evenings were reserved for a bath, laying out clothes for church and quiet games or a bedtime story. Then Mom developed a "crush" on Snooky Lanson, and I got my first taste of popular music. *Your Hit Parade* had its television debut in July 1950 as a summer replacement for *Robert Montgomery Presents.* Prior to that date, it had been a long-running radio program featuring singing greats like Frank Sinatra, Buddy Clark and Doris Day. But in 1949 the show's musical conductor, Mark Warnow, died, and the future of *Your Hit Parade* was uncertain.

The fate of the program was settled when Raymond Scott, Warnow's half-brother, took over the baton and brought his orchestra and a brand-new cast of singers and dancers to an eager TV audience.

The program's format on TV was essentially unchanged from radio, with singers presenting the seven most popular songs for that

particular week. According to *Your Hit Parade* producers, the songs were truly the people's choice, and were selected from ongoing surveys of radio stations, sheet-music sales and jukebox selections.

Snooky Lanson was one of the program regulars. He and Russell Arms were handsome lead singers, and the ladies loved them.

They didn't just sing. They actually "acted out" the songs, and they frequently shared the spotlight with songbirds Gisele MacKenzie and Dorothy Collins.

Your Hit Parade was sponsored by Lucky

Left to right: Russell Arms, Gisele MacKenzie, Dorothy Collins and Snooky Lanson.

Strike cigarettes, and each program started off with the theme song *Lucky Day*. According to author Bruce Elrod, who had once interviewed Snooky Lanson, the sponsor stipulated in each singer's contract that if they smoked, they were to smoke only Lucky Strikes.

Mom didn't smoke, but I remember her buying Dad those special, gift-wrapped cartons of Lucky Strikes for Christmas. I sort of guessed it had something to do with Snooky Lanson and the sponsor of *Your Hit Parade*.

Gisele, Russell (on the drum) and Snooky. Mom adored Snooky!
Photographs courtesy of Saturday Matinee, Hollywood, Calif.

Your Hit Parade enjoyed as much success as any musical program on radio or television. The reason, I think, is twofold. First, the cast was so clean-cut and enthusiastic. And second, the music was singable, with catchy tunes and lyrics, the sort of music you found yourself humming, the sort of music that entire families could sing together around a piano.

And that elicits another memory from my childhood. Our piano. Mom had always wanted one, though she was only able to play the easier arrangements. By 1952, she had saved enough money to purchase a secondhand upright. She gave my older brother Fred piano lessons and a Big Note songbook called *Your Hit Parade Favorites*.

I learned the words to *How Much Is That Doggie in the Window?*, *Mr. Sandman* and *Shrimp Boats*. Fred and I performed for

neighbors, relatives and, occasionally, just ourselves. It was a lot of fun, and it gave me a special love for popular music. In fact, I was still singing *Mr. Sandman* when my peers were grooving to the "new" sound of rock and roll.

Not long ago, while looking through some family keepsakes, I came across a letter my mother had received from Snooky Lanson. I suppose she must have written him as a fan, and being gracious, he had replied. The letter was warm and personal, just like the program.

Snooky told Mom that the cast rehearsed from Tuesday through Saturday and that they had to be very, very prepared because a live performance meant you had to perform flawlessly, or be clever enough to cover your mistakes.

Of course, I was too young to know whether Snooky, Gisele, Russell or Dorothy missed a cue or loused up the lyrics.

But I can't believe it happened often because the cast was made up of professionals, and they loved the music they were singing. The cast of *Your Hit Parade* presented their last performance in 1959.

Rock and roll was quickly becoming the rage with national audiences, but The American Tobacco Company was also introducing a new cigarette called Hit Parade. The sponsor thought they needed a new image to accompany their new product. It was a fatal mistake, for a new cast, a new format and a new cigarette couldn't keep the old allegiance. Both the cigarette and the program went up in smoke on Aug. 30, 1974.

I can still remember the lyrics of *Your Hit Parade's* closing song, though I doubt I'll ever be able to recall the tune: "So long for a while, that's all the songs for a while. So long from *Your Hit Parade* and the beautiful music we played."

What a wonderful memory! What a wonderful show! ❖

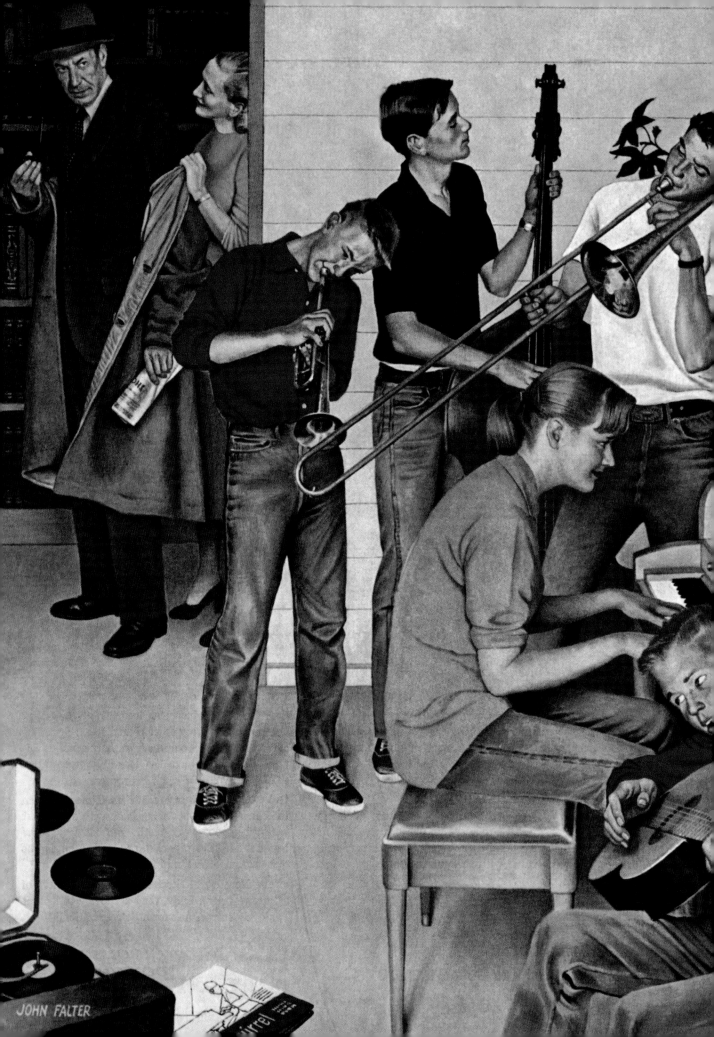

JOHN FALTER

Let's Dance

By Gail Marie Golden

"Come on, girls, we need to get busy." Mom and her two sisters always helped their mother clean on Saturdays, but this was a special Saturday. Everyone in the neighborhood took turns having the Saturday-night dance at their home, and it was their turn. As Mom retells the story, I can almost picture the hustle and bustle. I can see Grandma, working her daughters hard that morning and making sure the house was spotless—and I do mean *spotless.*

After the housework was done, Grandma began baking. First she made the pies—apple, cherry, chocolate and Mom's favorite, custard. Then, for the children, she baked some cookies. There would be oatmeal, ginger and usually some iced sugar cookies.

After the desserts were done, she would get out her biggest pots and start making chili, soup, or maybe stew. Oh, the house smelled so good that day! The other

They moved all the living-room furniture to make the dance floor.

ladies on the block brought in the rest of the meal. It was always fun to see what they made, because each had something she made best, and that was what they brought on the dance night—their best salad, best vegetable or best potato dishes, plus all the homemade bread you could eat!

Mom's father and her brother did the outside work—mowing, raking and sweeping off the porches. Her brother, being young and still afraid of girls, wasn't as excited as she was about the dance. He did like to have the other boys over, though, to play marbles and tag.

Later, after the yard was done, they came in and moved all the living-room furniture out of the way to make the dance floor. They set up a long table made of two sawhorses and a piece of plywood. Then her mother covered it with one of the best tablecloths.

Later in the day, folks started rolling in, bringing more food. The atmosphere was festive; it was one day of the week people were always in a good mood. The work week was over, houses cleaned and yard work done. Now was the time to relax, enjoy and socialize.

Now, don't think this was for adults only. Nope, where the parents went, so did the children. This was a family affair, and everyone had a good time. There were kids playing inside and kids playing outside, but no kids playing inside and outside. One thing you did not do at Grandma's house was run in and out.

1942 Richard Hudnut Salon ad, House of White Birches nostalgia archives

In one corner of the living room, the musical instruments began to stack up. There was always a fiddle or two, plus guitars, mandolins, banjos, washboards and whatever else anyone wanted to play. The children found it fun to go in the living room and look at the instruments, but they dared not touch; all the children knew that rule.

At last, it would be time to eat. The children were lucky because they got their plates fixed first. If weather permitted, they would take their plates out to the back yard, eating and playing, having a good time.

After the meal, the men would go into the living room and warm up their instruments while the women got the dishes done. Then the fun would begin. Everyone danced, adults and children alike, and they all had so much fun.

After a couple of hours of dancing and singing, it would be time for refreshments. Out came the desserts and coffee, tea or lemonade.

The house would shake from the music and dancing; you could hear the laughter a block away. My mom enjoyed the fact that the children got to stay up later than usual. But all too quickly, bedtime came, and each mother would take her child into the bedroom. The girls had to share their beds with all the other little girls there, and their brother had to do the same with the boys. There were so many that they had to lie crossways so they would all fit.

The children would lie in bed and tell stories for a long time. Some would drift off, but others had to be told to go to sleep. If I know my mom, she was one of the ones who had to be told.

Their parents would dance and sing all night. Come morning, everyone would wake their children, take them home, have a nice breakfast and start the day. Parents took a nap before church if they had time; if not, they waited until after church. These dances were one of the few forms of entertainment they had back then. The fun they had those Saturday nights remains with Mom to this day.

Such occasions were memorable for a little girl back in the '20s. Today our children get to do so much more, and yet the pleasure lasts so short a time. Families seem to want to go their separate ways and do their own thing. Many have lost sight of the joy in being together as a family.

Parents who believe in doing things together are making memories. I know Mom and her family shared such great memories with each other and all of their neighbors at those Saturday night dances back in the Good Old Days. ❖

When Music Was Real

By Doris Brecka

House parties were popular with rural folks throughout the 1920s and well into the 1930s. Even after the Crash of 1929, house parties were an affordable form of entertainment.

These neighborhood affairs were held during the weeks after the crops were in and before fieldwork was due to start. Snow-covered country roads were often unfit for driving on party nights, but guests were undeterred. They dressed warmly, grabbed a lantern and hiked the mile or so to the host family's home.

Along with several other children, I was usually just an observer, though occasionally a grown-up would draw us into the festivities. Often an old-time

Photo courtesy Library of Congress, FSA-OWI Collection

fiddler furnished the music. If the party was held in the parlor, most of the furniture would be removed and the carpet rolled up. Occasionally the party was held in a large kitchen with a plain wooden floor. This worked well, too.

Sometimes there were enough people present for a set of square dancers. Otherwise, a lively circle two-step could accommodate any number of dancers, as did the schottische. The more timid favored the old-time waltz, but it was no slow dance!

Taking just a few minutes off now and then for liquid refueling, the musicians played on and on. There usually was a midnight break for sandwiches and cake, brought in by the neighbors, plus coffee and whatever the hostess had prepared.

As farms became larger and farm homes boasted improvements like wall-to-wall carpeting, and as other forms of recreation became available, these neighborhood dances all but disappeared. A few of the excellent self-taught musicians joined larger groups that played in nearby halls.

My cousin was one of these musicians. He received his first accordion from a mail-order catalog when he was 4, and by age 13 or 14, he had become an accomplished musician.

His surprising talent may have been inherited; several of his uncles were musicians too. It was said that one of them wore out an accordion in three nights playing for a wedding celebration in the old country!

My cousin formed a dance band with a piano player and saxophonist. They played at nearly all the wedding dances in the area. Traditionally, they serenaded the newlyweds with *I Love You Truly* as the couple circled the floor alone. *Don't Sit Under the Apple Tree* brought memories of early wartime years. *Goodnight Sweetheart* and *Goodnight Little Girl of My Dreams* signaled the approach of the evening's end, and *Home, Sweet Home* made it definite to the regretful dancers.

When I asked my cousin if each musician was paid $3 or $4 for the evening's work, he said that it was $2 at first. It was a labor of love.

For many years, his band played on Saturday nights in local halls or in other communities nearby. Even after retiring, he continued to play music in a nursing home, bringing much pleasure to the residents.

I guess there were bad times in the Good Old Days, but an evening of dancing to a local band wasn't one of them. It created unforgettable memories for many of us. ❖

House Parties

*By Vera Brandt
as told to Lorna Brandt*

Back in the 1930s, we enjoyed occasional evenings of entertainment in the form of "house parties." Relatives, neighbors and friends would gather at the farmhouse for dancing in the living room or dining room, whichever had the larger floor space. The furniture from that room was moved to another room, and any floor covering—usually linoleum—was rolled up and taken outside.

Even the winter cold and snow in Ida County, Iowa, didn't stop us from having a good time. It wasn't unusual to find the rolled-up linoleum resting outside on a snowbank.

At first we used a bobsled and horses to get to the parties in the winter. In later years we had the luxury of traveling in a Model T Ford. There was no heater in the car, so we covered up with horsehide robes just as we had in the bobsled.

In freezing weather, as soon as we arrived at the party, each driver drained the water out of the radiator to avoid a frozen radiator later. We didn't have antifreeze in those days. When it was time to go, they had to fill the radiators with water again.

The entire family usually attended these parties. Here the children learned to dance by watching the adults, and the adults were quick to dance with the youngsters. When little eyes grew weary, the children were lined up on beds and lulled to sleep by the muffled sounds of music and visiting from the other room. During the cold winter, when all the guests' coats were piled on the bed or a couch, the children used the coats to cover up and keep warm. At one party, several coats had been tossed onto the couch before the host announced, "Oh, boys, you're putting your coats on Mother!" The host's mother had been sleeping on the couch.

The dance music was primarily provided by an accordionist. My mother's youngest brother played the accordion for many house parties. Sometimes a friend of his would come along, and they would take turns playing. Other times, another friend would play the violin to accompany the accordion.

The dances themselves were mostly two-steps, waltzes, schottisches and square dances. Sometimes the women lined up on one side of the room, and the men lined up on the other side. They walked toward one another and paired off with whomever was across from them.

While a couple was dancing, another person could come along and tap the shoulder of one of the couple to "rob" the partner. The person whose shoulder had been tapped had to give up his partner to the other person. Usually the men did the robbing.

A meal usually was served around midnight. For wedding or anniversary dances, someone would have prepared special "caps" for the honored couple in advance. Then they would "cap" the couple, and that couple would dance the first dance after the meal. At my parents' 10th anniversary, their caps consisted of pillowcases tied on their heads, hanging down their backs. Little dolls were attached to the corners of the pillowcases. For our wedding dance, my sister constructed a beautiful cap of crepe paper for me, with long streamers hanging down the back. My husband's cap was also made of crepe paper, with a knot on the top, and it sat on his head like a stocking cap.

As time went on, more and more people got word of upcoming parties and invited themselves and their friends, until the parties started getting too large for our houses. As more community dance halls were constructed, we gradually made the change to the larger facilities.

But I'll never forget the many wonderful times we had at house parties back in the Good Old Days. ❖

The National Barn Dance

By Bill Miller

*I*t is Saturday night, and the crowd is gathering outside the Eighth Street Theater in Chicago. Each eager ticket holder has waited months to be part of the best barn dance show in the country, *The National Barn Dance*, and many have driven miles to be part of the audience and share in a live broadcast of their favorite program.

The curtain opens and the caller sings out "Swing your partner and around you go, then turn to the corner and do si do" to the sound of music from the stage of *The National Barn Dance*—cowbells clankin', hands a-clappin' and feet a-tappin' to the sounds of some mighty fancy fiddlin', smooth guitar strummin' and sweet mandolins playin' good old-fashioned country music.

As the dancers swing to these magical sounds, the program begins. The audience now knows the wait was worth it.

The first broadcast of *The National Barn Dance* created quite a stir among the station's many listeners. WLS was billed as a light classical music station and was the favorite station of music lovers everywhere. But on that Saturday night in April 1924, these tender, music-loving ears were assaulted by the devil-may-care fiddlers' rendition of *Turkey in the Straw*.

'Twas the beginning of a radio program that lasted more than 40 years and was enjoyed by millions of listeners across this land.

This first broadcast emanated from the Sherman Hotel in Chicago. Grace Wilson, "The Girl with a Million Friends,"

The always-popular Homer and Jethro, joined by Cousin Tilford, practice offstage before their set on The National Barn Dance.

was on hand in the mezzanine studio for this first broadcast of *The National Barn Dance*, and remained part of the cast for the next four decades.

The innkeeper of the Sherman Hotel, Ernest Byfield, became very unhappy with the public's enthusiasm about the broadcast. "If that phone doesn't stop ringing," he warned, "the station will have to put in its own phone line." That evening he had more than 400 calls. It was the birth of the country music era, which has never died.

A girlfriend of Al Capone, a singer at the Sherman Hotel's College Inn, was asked by the producer to be a guest on *Barn Dance*. Capone watched the performance with smiling approval and later asked the producer, with suggestive firmness, "Well, don't she get paid?" She did.

Hearing this, Grace Wilson, who was at least as talented and certainly better known to *Barn Dance* followers, spoke up with equally courteous firmness. Thereafter, a full talent payroll was established.

In 1928, WLS was purchased by *The Prairie Farmer*, a rural newspaper, and the station took on a rural format, giving planting information, weather reports and the current prices of cattle, hogs and sheep at the Chicago Livestock Market.

That same year, the Eighth Street Theater (which was considered to be jinxed), with its 1,200-seat capacity, became the home of *The National Barn Dance* and would remain so for the next 40 years. There were two sold-out shows every Saturday evening, at 7 p.m. and 9 p.m. *The National Barn Dance* played before a live audience of 1,200 paying customers.

George Gobel, a native Chicagoan and a member of the cast, once remarked, "You could walk down the street on a summer Saturday evening—because there was no air conditioning and all the windows were open—and hear *The Barn Dance* coming out of every window, filling the airwaves."

Many notable performers had been members of *The National Barn Dance* family: Red Foley, Gene Autry, Pat Buttrum, Patsy Montana, The Prairie Ramblers and Homer and Jethro. Lulu Belle and Scotty teamed up in 1934 and were married that same year. She always appeared in an old-fashioned frock and high-top shoes, with a ribbon in her hair, and always sang disarmingly honest ballads. But she was liked best for her little-girl upstartedness. Scotty tinkled a five-string banjo, once popular in the hills of North Carolina from whence he came. Scotty Wiseman was an educated hillbilly with a master's degree in English.

There was Red Blanchard from Pittsville, Wis., who hired on as the Texas Yodeler, and later acted as a court jester and emcee.

Enthusiastic spectators at The National Barn Dance, *the forerunner to* The Grand Ole Opry.

Woody Mercer was raised in cowboy country, Sulphur Springs, Ariz. Woody sang through six years at the University of Arizona, earning a law degree and establishing a business in Phoenix before coming to Chicago to pursue his first love, singing country music. Fancy cowboy shirts were "pure made-up," invented by Hollywood. Woody always performed in a simple plaid shirt of the $3.95 variety from the Montgomery Ward's catalog.

In contrast, Bob Atcher, billed as "Top Hand of the Cowhands," from Hardin County, Ky. (where Lincoln was born, and moonshine stills were part of the landscape), always wore elegant cowboy regalia. The gifted tenor's shirts were tailor-made with fancy embroidery and spangles at a cost of $250 apiece. The college graduate had a wardrobe of 100 of them, and he always appeared in his complete cowboy outfit. One

Halloween, WLS had a party, and Bob showed up in a business suit. Everybody flipped out.

There were other colorful stars in the cast. Capt'n Stubby and the Buccaneers, an instrumental and singing quintet, were a solid fixture in the WLS programming. There were Betty Ross, "The Girl with the Golden Hair and the Blues in Her Voice" (and a master's degree in biology); Colleen and Donna Wilson, "The Beaver Valley Sweethearts"; Dalph Hewitt; and Arkie, "The Arkansas Woodchopper."

Lola Dee enjoyed success as a country singer after trying for years as a jump singer using the name Lola Ameche.

One of the all-time favorite groups was Homer and Jethro, whose stock and trade was always hilarious hillbilly satire on city tunes—"How much is that hound dog in the winder? I do hope that flea bag's fer sale." One winter they introduced a parody of a popular yuletide ditty. Their version was entitled *All I Want for Christmas is My Upper Plate*. During the next several weeks, to their astonishment, dozens of upper plates (most slightly used) came in the mail. Fan mail was always substantial, and

they were always in demand to make personal appearances at state and county fairs.

During station breaks for commercials, square dancers entertained the audience with encouragement from the cast, who enjoyed the dancers. It was always a thrill for square dance groups to be invited to Chicago and become part of *The National Barn Dance*. They had competed for this opportunity at state and county fairs. They now would be onstage with their favorite entertainers—a memory to be savored forever.

In 1924, Chicago was the country music capital of the world, the granddaddy of them all, and it remained so for many years.

The first announcer, George D. May, quit WLS and moved to Nashville in October 1925. There he established *The National Barn Dance* using the same format—one act after another, performing for several hours. On Nov. 28, 1925, he launched a new show, and two years later renamed it *The Grand Ole Opry*.

The late Roy Acuff described country music's lure this way: "It's good stuff; it never wore out. It comes and goes, but we've never been bigger than we are now." ❖

Left: Colleen and Donna Wilson, the Beaver Valley Sweethearts. Above: During station breaks, whirling square dancers performed, here watched by Red Blanchard and Grace Wilson, the only two charter members of The National Barn Dance. *Facing page: Lulu Belle and Scotty, 20-year veterans of* The National Barn Dance, *were audience favorites.*

John Slobodnik

Our First Radio

By Mary E. Kidwell

I was 6 years old in 1925. We had suffered through a very nasty winter, and most of us in the family had had a severe attack of flu. My three brothers and my mother and father and I lived in an old house that had been "electrified" just a year earlier. We would not need coal-oil lamps sitting around any longer. However, Mother kept a couple just in case the electricity went off, as it was prone to do in those days.

Long, black electric wires hung from the ceiling in the center of each room, with a single socket and light bulb at the end of the wire. Wires were also stapled along the upper edge of the wide baseboards around each room. These weren't really necessary for plugging in appliances, for there were few of those back then.

Mother's mother and my father's father lived with us. Mother and Daddy and I slept in the room off the kitchen (my bed was an old World War I Army cot), while my brothers and Grandpa slept in the two upstairs rooms. Grandma, who was crippled with rheumatism, slept in the front room next to a large entrance hall.

"Good evening, folks. We are coming to you all the way from Kentucky."

No one ever used this hall to come into the house because it was inconveniently located at the wrong side of the house. Daddy used this hall to rebuild a Model-T engine one winter when it was too cold to work in the barn at the bottom of the hill, and Mother made Christmas taffy and stored it in the hall to keep it cool until Christmas Day. The weather was still cold. It was rainy outside when Daddy came home from work one night carrying a strange-looking, oddly shaped wooden box with a couple of knobs on what looked like the front of the box. Daddy moved an old square table against the wall and told us to finish our supper first.

After the dishes were washed, Grandpa brought a chair in for himself and a rocker for Grandma and told my brothers to sit on the floor and behave. He plugged in one wire to the extension cord along the wall and the other to a long piece of metal leaning against the corner.

Daddy turned the knobs and sound came into the room. Then a strange, drawling voice came on. "Good evening, folks. We are coming to you all the way from the hills of Kentucky, from Renfro Valley. Tonight we are going to entertain you with good old country music by the Renfro Valley Boys. Sit back, relax and enjoy an evening of music that can only come from Renfro Valley and the Renfro Valley Boys."

We could hear the guitars and fiddles tuning up in the background. Then, almost immediately, hillbilly music came out into the bedroom. What a beautiful sound!

Facing page: *Radio Memories* by John Slobodnik, House of White Birches nostalgia archives

Grandpa didn't say a word. He just stood up and walked out through the living room to the dining room. Then we heard the door shut. A few minutes later he came back inside, wet and a little chilled.

"John," he said. "I walked all the way around the house and didn't see a thing. Where are those men playing from? You can't make me believe the sound came from that box."

It took a lot of convincing to make Grandpa believe that such beautiful music could come from a box filled with wires. Grandma just sat and rocked and rocked and rocked, as she said, "Tch, tch, tch, nothing good will ever come from such a contraption as that!" She kept repeating this all evening.

It didn't take long for our whole family, Grandpa and Grandma included, to come home at night and sit down on chairs drawn up to listen to the beautiful Western or country music.

Grandpa hurried from his job at the town's water works and hurried to finish his dinner.

Even Grandma, who usually complained about her rheumatism to get out of helping with the dishes, would pitch in so we could all gather around the radio and listen to the news and music together.

Grandpa only lived a short time after that. But Grandma lived for many years and looked forward to the nights when she could hear the music with the rest of the family.

It wasn't long before the first soap operas started showing up in the daytime. She liked to listen to Stella Dallas and Ma Perkins, among many others. However, she never quite understood that it was only a show, and that these were actors and actresses playing parts. ❖

Below: The cast of the Renfro Valley Barn Dance. *This was the show the author and his grandparents listened to on their first family radio.*

Dancing by the Victrola

By Lee Hill-Nelson

Dance all night, Stay a little longer, Take off your coat, And throw it in the corner. These words from a song recorded by Bob Wills describe dances in West Texas during the late 1920s and 1930s. Some folks called them ranch dances; others called them country dances. But whatever their name, the Victrola made these dances happen.

Thomas A. Edison invented a phonograph machine in 1877. *Mary Had a Little Lamb* was the first tune played. Victrola became the trade name for the machine. A motor with a spring wound by a crank turned records and music played when the needle was set to the record.

By the 1930s, the Victor Company had improved on the invention. Some called it a "talking machine" or a "record player," but most everyone just said "Victrola."

Dances were the biggest social events in West Texas. If no musicians were available, or if there was no money to pay musicians, Victrolas played the music.

In *San Antonio Rose*, Dr. Charles Townsend described these dances: "When someone decided to give a dance at his ranch or farm, word was passed from neighbor to neighbor, by people on the streets or by telephone. On rare occasions, the dances were by special invitation, but most of the time everyone who met certain standards of conduct was invited (some came who did not). Often they included people in a small area, from adjoining farms or ranches, who usually could attend the dance and go home the same evening. The 'all night' dances brought more people from such a broad geographical area that they could not return home that night."

Whole families came as far as 60 miles by car. Others closer by rode in wagons or on horseback. The hostess prepared ahead of time by moving all the furniture out of the room except for the Victrola. Babies and small children shared the hostess' beds, some at the head of the bed, some at the foot. Older children danced or played games like dominoes or spin the bottle. Romances happened.

Not everyone owned a Victrola. Hardworking ranch and farm people thought a Victrola was a luxury during the Depression and Dust Bowl years. Those who had one shared it with friends and other families. Bud, my brother, married in 1933. Not only did he bring home a sister for me; she had a Victrola! I spent hours listening to *Red Sails in the Sunset*, while in my imagination I'd see a ship with red sails slowly move over the horizon of the blue Pacific Ocean.

Recently I asked my sister-in-law, Audrey, about her Victrola. "When Bud and I married, we lived close to Turkey, in a community of farms, not ranches," she recalled. "Many cousins lived nearby. We and our cousins pooled money to order records from catalogs, which always had two pages of records listed. We liked Bob Wills' music best of all." It is no wonder West Texans enjoy Bob Wills' music. When we listen, we hear the influence West Texas had on his music and lyrics. His music goes on and on, though nowadays not on the Victrola.

As farmers and ranchers from such places as Turkey, Estelline, Quitaque, Northfield and Matador battled dreary dust storms and the Great Depression, the Victrola gave them a social life with music. They danced all night and pitched their coats in the corner, just like Bob Wills sang. ❖

Dance Music

By Mildred Mitchell

*S*an Antonio Rose … I can hear it yet, ringing out through the open windows of Corwin's Opera House on summer evenings. In a town only five blocks long, including the residential section, I suppose a lot of people considered the music a miserable nuisance that they could live without. But to me and a lot of other teenagers, it was music straight from heaven.

In 1940 we danced. I was 18, living in a farming neighborhood 6½ miles from the little town of Marion, Mich. Saturday night was date and dancing night. If a girl had a date, they went someplace to dance. If we had no date and no transportation, we walked along with some other dateless girls to the nearest dance hall, which for us was in Marion. If we didn't dance on Saturday night, we felt that we had missed out on the most important night of our lives. Young girls can be very dramatic.

The upper floor of the oldest building in town had been an opera house in the early 1900s. It was pretty ramshackle by 1940, but the floor was smooth, and the stage still occupied the south wall. A potbellied stove warmed the place in winter, while windows opened to cool it in summer.

If we didn't dance on Saturday night, we felt we had missed out.

Music was supplied by local talent, usually with banjo, ukulele, fiddle and often one or two mouth organs. Then, in the summer of 1940, a group of laborers came in to harvest the big fields of string beans and cucumbers that were beginning to catch on with local farmers. One of the older men, a fellow called Mexican Mike, showed up at the dance hall one Saturday night, and the music changed forever. He could play a guitar, banjo, fiddle, anything you put in his hands—and he could sing.

Up until this point, we had contented ourselves with square dancing, round dancing, the schottische, the jitterbug and the Charleston, stamping our feet and clicking our heels and often making up the steps as we went along. Now we learned to glide, for with Mike leading, the music flowed smooth and steady. When Mexican Mike grew tired of picking or fiddling, he threw back his head and sang *San Antonio Rose*. If he ever sang any other song, I don't remember it.

San Antonio Rose became our melody of love, our song of romance, the heavenly sound that sent us into a dream world while we swooped and glided around the floor in the arms of our special lad of the moment. As 18-year-olds often do, I soon found myself waiting for one young man who always asked me to dance when *San Antonio Rose* was played or sung. It was only one or two dances a night and only the one song. The rest of the night, I found other partners, for he disappeared.

We know what 1941 brought. That war, which our farming fathers followed by listening to radios powered by car batteries, and which was far away in another country, became our war. One by one, our dance partners disappeared as our men volunteered or were drafted. Our brothers, cousins and young uncles all went away.

Some of my friends got diamond rings that Christmas, but not me. Saturday-night dances were still held in the opera house, but it wasn't the same.

The crowd dwindled and soon Mexican Mike was gone, too. The hall closed. Girls went to work in defense plants or married their sweethearts and followed their men around from camp to camp until the men were shipped overseas, some never to return. It was time to grow up, and we did.

For me it was the defense plant, where I learned more than how to build bombers. I had to learn about living in a big city, Detroit. It was a lot different than life on the farm, but like the old dancing on Saturday night, it was what we did. I envied my married friends and wondered what had happened to my *San Antonio Rose* dance partner. Perhaps I shed a tear or two whenever I heard *San Antonio Rose* on the radio.

Then, in 1942, as if by magic, he reappeared. And during a Christmas furlough, with *San Antonio Rose* blasting out on the car radio, I got a tiny diamond.

In March 2003 we celebrated our 60th wedding anniversary with our three children, 10 grandchildren and 15 great-grandchildren. Did the bandleader play *San Antonio Rose*? No! He had never heard of it. ❖

This western dance was held in McIntosh County, Okla., in 1940. Photo courtesy Library of Congress, FSA-OWI Collection.

Singalongs

By Pearl A. Franklin

Back when I was a youngster in the '40s, every Sunday night we would have a sing-along at our house. All the relatives came, each bringing a simple dish to pass. Mama always provided the coffee, tea and milk, and in winter she even had hot cocoa with marshmallows.

Mama would play the piano. She really didn't have to read the notes; she was so talented, she could play anything after just hearing it on the radio. At an early age, when she took lessons, she played so well that the piano teacher said Mama knew as much as she did, and she couldn't teach her any more.

At about 6 p.m., our relatives would gather in the living room around the piano. Grandma and Grandpa were there, too.

I had to stand on a stool so I could see. If I didn't, my nose would be on the piano keys. I always stood by Aunt Sue. She was nine years older than I was, and she always looked out for me.

We would sing hymns, the good old favorites. Papa would join Mama and play his mouth organ to accompany some of the songs. Together we sang *The Old Rugged Cross*, *Little Brown Church* and *Jesus Loves Me*; of course, I was good at *that* one! We also sang *Take My Hand Precious Lord* and *Near the Cross*.

I couldn't read, of course, but after a few Sundays, I could join in the chorus with the rest of them. We sang loud and lively, enjoying every minute. We didn't have neighbors close by, so we didn't bother anyone with our singing. And anyway, it sounded good!

One Sunday evening in particular, everyone cracked up in laughter. That was when I sang so proudly and loudly, "… till my ruptured

soul shall find rest beyond the river." Everyone had stopped singing, and they were looking at me and laughing. Mama even stopped playing, and she was laughing so hard she had tears in her eyes.

I must have looked quite puzzled. Then Mama reached out her arms and hugged me and said, "The word is '*raptured*,' not '*ruptured*,' Honey." After Mama had explained why everyone was laughing, I laughed too.

"The word is 'raptured,' not 'ruptured,' Honey," Mama said.

After singing, laughing and joking, the women set out the food on the sideboard. Mama had prepared a huge roast earlier for our Sunday dinner, and there were plenty of leftovers for our potluck meal. Nowadays a person can hardly afford that much meat. But back in the '30s, meat was not that expensive, and it went a long way.

When it was time to eat, we all lined up. Each of us took a plate from the stack on the small table next to the sideboard. Because I couldn't see the top of the sideboard, I would hold my plate in both hands and walk beside Aunt Sue. She told me what was there, and I would tell her what I wanted. Then, when my plate was full, she would help me to my seat. Once I was settled, she would go back and get her meal, then come back and sit with me.

When we were finished eating, we would go back for dessert. Every once in a while, someone would bring homemade ice cream made fresh that day in an ice-cream maker. What a treat, especially when Grapenuts were sprinkled on top! Yummy!

To this day, I cherish my memories of our sing-alongs, back in the Good Old Days when families got together and enjoyed down-to-earth fun. ❖

Alexander's Ragtime Band

By Margaret Gunn

High-school parties, good friends, fun and a simple, joyful time—that's what the song *Alexander's Ragtime Band* recalls for me. And I'm not the only one with wonderful feelings about that lilting tune. That song did a lot for me—but it did even more for its creator. Irving Berlin wrote the words and music, and it was his first giant hit. He earned the title "King of Ragtime," and this memorable song was in large part responsible for these accolades.

The movie *There's No Business Like Show Business* delighted me when I was a teenager. And the hit song of that movie, of course, was *Alexander's Ragtime Band*. That year, this favorite song of mine was No. 1, so many people shared my enthusiasm for the tune.

I have many cherished memories of growing up in Galena, Ill. A friend of mine who lived in a big house held dances for her teenage friends in the house's large attic. These were well-supervised events with lively music. The song I enjoyed so much was included at every dance.

A dear friend from those Galena days still keeps in touch with me with weekly phone calls. We live in neighboring states, and so I occasionally visit her. When I do, it saddens me to see her walking painfully with the aid of a cane. But then I recall with her *Alexander's Ragtime Band*, and her joyful, lively dancing to that tune. It is a gleeful recollection for both of us.

A fellow who lived in my Galena neighborhood had a band. It was a small group, not too

Alexander's Ragtime Band
© 1911 by Ted Snyder Co., Inc. New York

heavily booked for performances. But when the band was called upon to play at little social events, who do you suppose was its unpaid secretary? Me! This band often played a special tune because it was a "ragtime" band. Of course, the tune was *Alexander's Ragtime Band*.

There was no television in those long-ago days, but the radio provided entertainment that was much appreciated. Music was an important feature of those radio days, and I was always delighted when I heard my favorite song over the airwaves. I heard it often, so I knew that it was popular.

Many of my memories of *Alexander's Ragtime Band* were of the years before World War II. Later, during the war, there was nostalgia for the tune, as we recalled the days before the war. That music was played when soldiers were in our area, at parties where servicemen were being entertained. The words and the music gave a lift to any event.

Many memories from my girlhood seem to include *Alexander's Ragtime Band* in some way. Certainly the song is not linked with any unhappy event during my youth. The song is a musical insurance policy for good memories. It's a pleasure to recall all the times through the years that this tune brought me joy. It was a fun-and-games time—and tune—in my life.

We will always gratefully remember Irving Berlin and his music. His wonderful songs brought joy to many people the world over. He has been important in many of our lives. His *Alexander's Ragtime Band* will always be a treasured and valued part of mine. ❖

Grandma Led The Dance

By Eva R. Priestley

When I was very young, in the 1930s, life seemed gay and uncomplicated. We—my parents and my younger sister and I—lived in the suburbs. When company came the living room in our tiny home seemed to shrink remarkably. Extra chairs were pulled in to fit tightly around our big table, and sometimes the folded-up ironing board was laid across two stools to fashion a long bench for the younger children.

My mother had to perform something like a snake dance just to bring the food from the kitchen to the table. Many arms stretched out to help her position the bowls and platters so they were within reach of all the hungry relatives.

Sometimes when there were just too many of us, we also used the kitchen table. I liked that best because Grandma always sat with us kids in the kitchen. When my Uncle Willy joined us, it was doubly fun. Uncle Willy and Grandma made it seem like a kitchen party, and they saw to it that we had our plates filled with only the food we liked. Had our tiny house been bigger with a formal dining room, we never would have been able to enjoy such togetherness!

As soon as everyone was fed and the dishes had been cleared away, my aunts and uncles and cousins pushed the chairs to the side and carried the living-room table into the bedroom. To me, the resulting space seemed enormous.

Then, as a rule, Uncle Willy and Uncle Gary would bring in their accordions, and my father would get his harmonica out of the drawer. Our house musicians assembled in one corner, a bit out of the way. While they tuned up and tried

to decide what to play, Grandma's feet tapped in anticipation, and Grandpa leaned back in his chair and gave her his amused grin.

"Let's have a nice polka," suggested Grandma. "Or a waltz. Anything that sounds good."

A polka it was. Polkas always came first. It was a tradition. It was also tradition that my mother got to dance with Grandma first. Both of them kicked up their heels nicely, and sometimes onlookers had to quickly move their legs so they wouldn't get hit by dancing feet.

It was a tradition that my mother got to dance with Grandma first.

Eventually each of us kids got a turn to dance with Grandma. Then the big and small cousins tried it together—right foot, left foot, and a hop and a twirl. Even my crowd-shy sister participated and whooped for joy.

Aunts and uncles joined in the fun, and soon everyone was bumping into each other. There simply were too many of us in that little space. Then some people had to move out into the hallway to sway and swirl.

As best as I can remember, Grandma never missed a dance, and Grandpa always sat back and just watched the gaiety.

When our musicians were finally tired of playing, a few grown-ups quickly brought in the table again and rearranged the chairs. Then my tired mother had to dish up more food so nobody would go home hungry.

Our family ties were strong in those Good Old Days, and with not much to amuse us, we made our own entertainment.

Grandma departed from us decades ago, but memories of her linger on. I hope her happy genes and her love for dancing will never be lost in future generations. ❖

My Father's Fiddle

By Florence Cardinal

*D*uring the Great Depression, with money scarce and the living anything but easy, hardworking people sought ways to add to meager incomes. I remember my father packing up his fiddle in its battered black case and heading out to play at a country dance. With faithful old Dollie and Robin hitched to the wagon or sleigh, he would take off to pick up neighbors with guitars, accordions and banjos.

Many of the dances took place in local halls or schools. But sometimes the musicians had to leave home after an early supper to travel to a dance 10 or 20 miles away.

Then Dad would return, nodding off on the wagon seat, just as the morning sun gilded the barn roof. He would unhitch and feed his tired horses, then drag himself into the house on weary feet, take his fiddle from its case and hang it on the wall beside his rocking chair. After he handed Mother the dollar or two he had earned for his night's labor, he was off to the barn to milk the cows.

Dad would return just as the morning sun gilded the barn roof.

Mother and I often accompanied Dad to nearby dances. These were truly family affairs, attended by everyone from babes in arms to their octogenarian grandparents. When the guitars tuned up and Dad tucked his old fiddle under his chin, people of all ages streamed onto the dance floor. I don't know which I learned first—how to walk or how to waltz. I'll never forget that shiver of delight I experienced when Dad's bow touched the strings.

There was lots of socializing going on in the background during those dances. Neighbors took advantage of these get-togethers to visit and admire the new babies. There was ample opportunity for farmers to trade equipment or marshal help for a barn-raising. When the ladies weren't dancing, they picked up their knitting or embroidery. Their hands were seldom idle as they traded recipes and gossip with neighbors they hadn't seen for weeks.

At midnight, the dancing came to a halt for a potluck lunch of sandwiches prepared with home-baked bread, frosted cakes and freshly baked cookies, all washed down with hot coffee. The musicians and the dancers welcomed the refreshing break. By 1 a.m., with the leftovers packed away in boxes to take back home and the floor swept and dusted with fresh wax, the dancing began again. It continued until 3 or 4 in the morning.

As youngsters grew weary and their small eyelids began to droop, they retired to piles of soft coats in the cloakroom where they slept soundly. Grandmas, grandpas and even parents moved back into the corners to visit, doze or nod to the music as the younger people took over the dance floor.

Many marriages began there as romances when handsome young men twirled full-skirted young ladies in an old-time waltz or schottische. A stolen kiss on the front steps, a whispered word, and two hearts became entwined for life.

A few months later, Dad would be asked to play for a wedding dance.

Weather seldom hindered the festivities. The dancers came on hot summer nights when the skies were ablaze with stars.

They came on rainy nights, arriving with soggy coats draped over their heads and dripping hems that left small puddles on the floor.

They came during spring breakup when mud-spattered clothing was removed in the cloakroom. Like butterflies emerging from a cocoon, brightly colored skirts and shirts appeared from brown paper packages where they'd been tucked safely away for the treacherous trek to the hall.

The determined dancers came in winter through snowdrifts so deep that they threatened to upset the sleigh, and often did.

They came on nights when the mercury plummeted far below zero and the night air grew foggy with the breath of a dozen people wrapped in quilts and blankets as they burrowed deep into straw-filled sleigh beds.

Only real blizzards caused a cancellation. Blowing snow could make visibility nearly impossible. No one wanted to risk getting lost and freezing to death in the icy chill of winter's blast.

In my mind's eye, I still see those country dances … checkered shirts and a rainbow of flared skirts … pink-cheeked babies and sun-wizened old-timers. I can still hear the twang of the guitars, the resonant notes of the accordion and, above all, the voice of Dad's fiddle playing *The Devil's Dream* or *The Missouri Waltz. Turkey in the Straw, Irish Washerwoman, Life in the Finland Woods*—Dad played them all on that old fiddle.

His old fiddle hangs on my bedroom wall, and I hear his music every time I pass one of the halls where he used to play.

The author's father, Fred Parker, and his fiddle.

The music holds the whole experience together for me with a magical fairyland glue.

I hummed those catchy tunes as I gathered eggs and washed dishes. I still find myself humming them today as I do my household chores.

I recall other times, though, when Dad would tuck that battered instrument under his chin and play classics like *Brahms' Lullaby, Blue Danube Waltz, Handel's Messiah* and *Schubert's Serenade.*

Those were the times when that old fiddle became a far more sophisticated instrument. It became a violin.

My father passed away 10 years ago at the age of 79. I wrote this story as a tribute to a man I loved deeply and will always miss. His old fiddle hangs on my bedroom wall, and I hear his music every time I pass one of the halls where he used to play.

Late at night, I imagine I can hear *Brahms' Lullaby* as I drift off to sleep. His music will always live on in my memory. ❖

The Summer Dance

By Ruth Brownfield

The year was 1935, and I had just graduated from high school. As usual, I was spending the summer with my aunt and her husband who owned a grocery store and meat market. They paid me, and that year I made enough money to put myself through beauty school in the fall when I went back home to Illinois.

The place was Shelby, a small town in Indiana with a population of 450–500 people. There were only the grocery, a miscellaneous store, post office, small restaurant, church, one garage and one place that repaired farm machinery. Shelby was about 18 miles south of Crown Point, Ind.

Each summer, the influx of people who had cabins along the Kankakee River helped increase income for the few businesses. The river was a short distance from town and was used for baptisms as well as swimming and small boats.

There wasn't much to do for entertainment except the Saturday-night dances. Everyone looked forward to them. They were held on the third floor of the miscellaneous store, which had hardwood floors, big windows, and a stage for the band.

You could attend as a couple or stag, and it cost 50 cents per person. The band, Cy Wright and His Four Lefts, played on a radio station in Gary, Ind. They really were good. They could play music for the usual dances like waltzes and fox-trots, and they'd play for square dancing and round dancing every once in a while. One night my girlfriend and I were asked to square dance by two fellows who were at least 6 feet tall. We were only about 5 feet, 5 inches. Since it was my last night before going home, I decided to wear my white prom dress and high-heeled white shoes.

Then came the most embarrassing moment of my life. The two fellows joined hands and we girls joined hands and had to put them over the fellows' necks. When the fellows started spinning, it wasn't long before I was hanging almost straight out. Out went one of my shoes through the window! I had to yell "Stop!" and the dance ended. My shoe landed high heel down on the head of a guy I knew. Some of his friends were standing there talking to him when it hit, and they couldn't believe their eyes.

It wasn't long before they all came upstairs holding my shoe and wanting to know who the

Photo courtesy Library of Congress, FSA-OWI Collection

"striptease girl" was. My face turned as red as a beet. Did they ever have fun kidding me!

Shortly thereafter, the band started playing *Goodnight, Irene*, as it was midnight. Dances usually started at 8 p.m. and lasted until midnight. Everyone always hated to hear that song since it meant that it was time to go. Since my middle name was Irene, I hated to hear it too.

I always said I would never marry a man who didn't dance, but guess what? I married someone who had two left feet and never did learn. So that ended my dancing, too. ❖

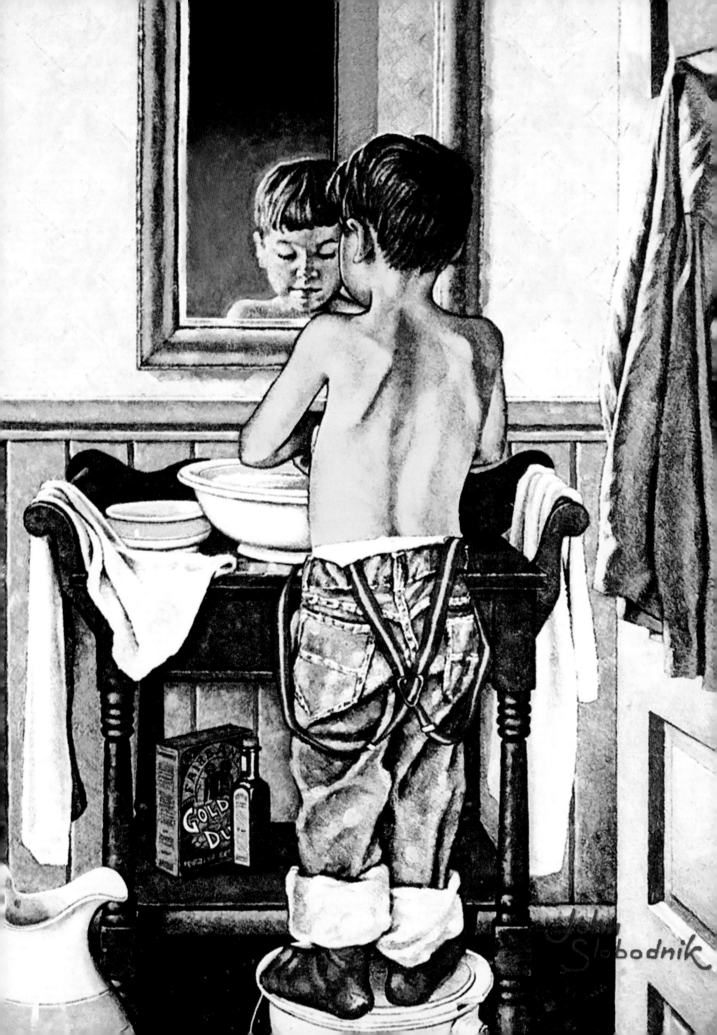

Wonderful Sundays

Chapter Five

There is no way we could leave the topic of Saturdays in the Good Old Days without looking at that other very important day of the weekend. Sunday was a day of rest and rejuvenation, a day when chores were cut back to a minimum. It was a day for all things spiritual and many things social.

It was also a day indelibly tied to Saturday since the "goin' to meetin'" day engendered the dreaded Saturday night bath.

It's hard to imagine today not having plenty of running water and a bathtub or shower in which you could luxuriate on a daily basis. But it really hasn't been that long since the weekly bath was a fact of life.

Our little home didn't have running water until I was 11 or 12. Even then, during some of the drought years, you didn't take it for granted there would be water in your well or cistern, so conservation even after the advent of pressurized water was an imperative.

Now, that's not to say we went around dirty (even though little boys like me would have preferred it that way). No, we had basin baths to tide us over until Saturday night.

Then, out came the galvanized tub and kettle after kettle of steaming water. The object was to get the water as hot as the first bather could stand so the last bather wouldn't have to break the ice! That may be an exaggeration, but being the next-to-youngest, and therefore the next-to-last in that tub, it sometimes felt that cold to me.

There is an old saying: "Don't throw the baby out with the bath water." I've heard lots of theories as to the origin of this proverb. I still think it comes from the Saturday night bath. By the time the baby of the family was bathed, you wanted to make sure you didn't forget to get the young sprout out of that murky water.

Not one time do I remember my baby sister being thrown out with the bath water, even though there probably were times I wish she had.

> *Not one time do I remember my baby sister being thrown out with the bathwater.*

The next morning reminded me why the Saturday night bath was worth suffering through.

Ah, wonderful Sundays! Yes, some chores were inevitable. Cows still had to be milked and livestock fed. But that quickly faded into the preparation for church and Sunday afternoon socializing.

I didn't mind Sunday school and church at all. I liked learning about the Lord. I figured that Anyone who told us to rest one day out of seven was worth listening to.

Then came Sunday dinner, that wondrous meal loved by kids and ministers alike. Usually we gathered at my paternal grandparents' home along with dozens of others from my large, extended family. There was nothing like a shared Sunday afternoon to bond families and friends together.

It didn't matter where Sunday afternoons took us, the hours flew by like a hummingbird headed for a hollyhock. Sunday was soon spent, and all that was left was a wistful wish that there had been a way to hold onto the weekend for just a little while longer.

School days and work days loomed ahead. It would be a whole week until we were rescued by super Saturdays and wonderful Sundays.

—*Ken Tate*

Splish, Splash!

By Jean Powis

ake a bath. It's Saturday night." That's what my mother used to say in the 1940s to five offspring who waited for their turns to soak in the family bathtub. Soak isn't what happened, though. It was more like a quick dip, lather, rinse and get out clean. Our home had no hot running water, so my parents had to laboriously fill the tub with water heated in pots and pans on our kitchen stove. My most vivid memory of that cookware was the old, hammered aluminum teakettle. With its shiny surface, it was in continuous use on bath night.

When the tub was half full of hot and cold water, the oldest of five youngsters enjoyed a warm bath. The rest of us shivered in the cooling water. We were fair in not overdoing our tub time—except for one sister who would lock the bathroom door and hog the hot water.

Mom tried to keep the water warm by pouring water from the tea-kettle into the tub after each child dried off with a towel kept warm on the bathroom radiator. But being the youngest and the last to take part in the Saturday ritual, I had to dunk in lukewarm water and put up with ugly rings of soap scum that coated the sides of the tub.

One sister would lock the bathroom door and hog the hot water.

Lucky Mom and Dad had their baths on Wednesdays.

Years later, when we had a hot-water tank installed and could bathe at our leisure, I used to stay in the tub until my skin wrinkled.

Our family bathtub was a handsome cast-iron, porcelain-finish, claw-foot model. It still proudly stands in the family home, which is now occupied by my sister.

Even with the water situation, my family was fortunate, because having a bathtub in the home was a luxury in the 1940s. Most of our neighbors, relatives and friends bathed in a round or oval galvanized tub. Our next-door neighbor used the oval model. When not in use, it was hung on a large nail in the wall behind their living-room wood-stove. Sunday night must have been bath time in their house, because during the summer, when house windows were open, we could hear the clinking of the tub handles as it was apparently put into use.

Modern bathroom conveniences eventually replaced their silver oval wonder, leaving it as a bathtub for their dog. Watching their dog get his weekly cleaning was fun, but if we didn't back away from him when he shook to dry off, we'd get soaked.

After the dog died, the galvanized receptacle was used as a planter in the summer and a storage bin for garden equipment in the winter. That tub was a marvel. It still exists, serving as an improvised swimming pool for the neighbor's grandchildren.

Facing page: *Saturday Night Bath* by Charles A. MacLellan © 1916 SEPS: Licensed by Curtis Publishing

My grandfather told my family about the summer bathing routine of his youth. When it started to rain, he and his brother would take off their clothes and run outside with a bar of soap, using the pelting raindrops as a shower. Different, for sure—but not very warm!

In those days, another neighbor did his bathing at the city's public indoor baths. There were two or three of these facilities in my hometown, as there were in nearby communities and other areas of the United States.

Most of these baths surfaced between 1890–1915, not only for personal cleanliness, but also as a symbol of good character for the middle class and as an amenity for those less fortunate. Generally, each community bath consisted of hot- and cold-water showers and a large swimming pool with 75- to 80-degree temperatures.

The popularity of these baths peaked in the early 1900s when facilities in Albany, N.Y., a city near my home, saw as many as 800 visitors annually enjoy their refreshing waters. For 10 cents in Albany's Public Bath No. 2, each bather received a towel and a bar of soap, and was required to take a hot shower before entering the pool for a dip. The water was continuously changed in the pool, which was referred to as "the plunge," with fresh water running in and out. Plunge water was changed completely every two weeks in the summer and every three in the winter. Wearing a bathing suit or trunks was a must, and no one who was ill was allowed in the plunge.

The public baths were open every day except Sundays and holidays. A schedule separating males and females was maintained, and a "no boisterous behavior" rule was strictly enforced. Bathers were allowed to stay in the pool for no longer than 30 minutes at a time, and the use of tobacco and the entrance of dogs were forbidden.

Public baths no longer exist in my hometown, but Albany residents still use their only remaining open bath, Public Bath No. 2. They pay a slightly higher usage fee, and towel and soap are no longer provided. Nonetheless, last year, more than 5,000 bathers made use of the bath's hot shower and invigorating plunge water.

When I went to my aunt's house for a vacation in the summer, I bathed in the nearby lake. Hot sunny days were my thing because that spring-fed lake was cold. If I balked at bathing in the lake, my aunt would fill her large kitchen sink with heated water, mix it with cold, and lift me into its warm water. I liked that bath. It meant not having to wait for siblings to bathe before me.

Of course, nothing but 21st-century plumbing would do for me today. But it's somewhat mundane compared to taking a bath in the Good Old Days. ❖

Saturday-Night Bath

By Barbara Deming

It's funny how deprived some people make themselves out to be. They feel poor because they don't drive a new or expensive car, can't shop at Neiman Marcus, or are unable to live in an exclusive area of town. They have never experienced what it means to survive on so little and still not feel underprivileged.

Growing up happily in the 1940s, in small-town Texas, I never knew we were poor. There were hundreds of other families right there with us, so we never felt isolated. We all had enough to eat, clean clothes to wear, a good public-school education, and plenty of love and laughter. And a bath every Saturday night.

That trusty old No. 3 washtub in which Mama had once boiled diapers—the same tub that was used to gather vegetables from the garden and ice down watermelon in the summer—was the very same washtub we used for a bathtub on Saturday night.

Kettles of water were heated on the nearby stove. A kitchen chair was drawn up to hold the Ivory soap in a dish and a sweet-smelling, sun-dried towel. The Philco radio was tuned to *Jack Benny*, *The Lone Ranger* or *The Green Hornet*. With shades drawn down and doors securely closed for privacy, each person in the family leisurely enjoyed the Saturday-night bath, "whether we needed it or not." ❖

The End of Dirt

By Lorna M. Kaine

Every day I step out of my shower, clean. Taking a shower is part of my routine, something I take for granted. I remember taking baths the old-fashioned way, in a galvanized tub, sharing bathwater with my sister in a steamy kitchen on a Saturday night.

In those days, getting dirty was serious—especially if the dirt was still visible on Sunday morning after the Saturday bath. It was an affront to God to enter His house in anything less than pristine condition. So we were especially careful to remain clean after our Saturday-night bath.

We squirmed through breakfast, slipped into our starched dresses and twiddled our thumbs till it was time to go to church.

Walking to Sunday school was fraught with hazards. We took the shortest path, which happened to parallel the railroad tracks. The way was covered with oily cinders, and once in a while, a train chugged past us, its engine blowing black smoke. It was not unusual for me to arrive at church with a dark streak on my face (the result of spit misapplied by my sister to a black spot) and sooty flecks on my dress. White summer shoes were always a disaster. Their polish never lasted the walk on the cinders.

It did not help that I was the only person who seemed to suffer this fate. Other family members who walked with me arrived at church looking as good as they did when they left the house. After several thousand scoldings from my mother for not being careful, I closed my ears and decided that being dirty was comfortable, and I was going to enjoy it.

Fate intervened in the form of new plumbing in our house. We had always had running water, but now we had a bathtub and a hot-water tank. It was now possible to take a bath any old time. The Saturday-night ritual turned into an every-night routine. And now that we had a hot-water tank, doing the laundry became a lot easier, too. Getting my clothes dirty was no longer a major calamity, and it was no longer a big deal to arrive at church on Sunday morning in smudgeless condition.

Today when my friends and I reminisce about all the changes that have occurred during our lifetimes, we mention television, air travel, space exploration and computers. Seldom does anybody mention bathtubs. But sometimes, after a hard day's work in my yard and garden, I see remnants of the little girl who left the Saturday-night bath inky, and I smile. Although these memories bring back difficult times, I treasure them because they are uniquely mine. They do, however, wash off. After a hot shower and shampoo, I turn back into a responsible adult—till the next time. ❖

Washtub Bathroom

By Lilli M. Baxter

Behind the chairs all draped with clothes,
We scrubbed a week of grime.
The stove got hot on where we sat;
Must keep turning all the time.

The kids all waited for their turn,
All seven plus Mom and Pop.
By the time we kept the water clean,
We all felt ready to drop.

But Saturday was that night of nights,
When all our world came clean,
To start a world all fresh and new
'Til Saturday—same old scene.

When everyone had clean long johns on,
And ready to jump into bed,
No one forgot their "Lay me downs,"
For a blessing must be said.

Saturday Night On the Farm

By Jean Cailliau

In the early 1930s, one of the best parts of a weekend visit to my grandparents' farm was the Saturday-night bath. It ranked right up there with sleeping between goose-down comforters and watching the frost on the insides of the tall, narrow windows sparkle in the starlight while I blew steamy breath into nowhere. It was always so cold in the upstairs bedroom of Grandpa's farmhouse!

During the day, we spent our time outside, all bundled up in snowsuits against the cold. Mine was warm gray wool with green pine trees appliqued on the front, and I wore a cap that fit over my ears and was always tied too tightly under my chin. For extra warmth, a long scarf was wrapped around my neck. It covered my nose and mouth on its way to the tops of my knee-high boots. Sometimes I felt like I could hardly move.

When evening came and dinner dishes were back in the cupboards, Grandma brought out the round galvanized washtub, the same tub we swam in all summer. My aunt pushed the tub right in front of the cookstove that had heated buckets of water while we ate dinner. It was fun to watch the steaming water splash into the big tub.

My cousin and I both fit in the tub at the same time. We tried to hold the splashing to a minimum, but that's hard to do if you are 4 or 5 years old. But Mom and my aunt were good sports; they let us soak for a while before they brought the big bars of homemade soap to finish the job.

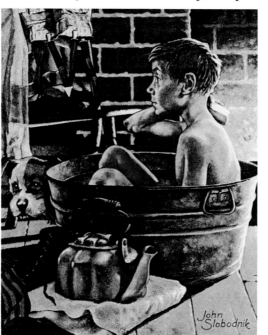

Saturday Night Bath by John Slobodnik, House of White Birches nostalgia archives

After a good scrub-down, we jumped out of the warm water and into a waiting towel. Just a little damp, we pulled on our new flannel pajamas. Still giggling, we each ate a biscuit left from supper and drank a juice glass of milk that had tiny chunks of yellow floating on the top. My aunt called it buttermilk and said it would make us sleepy.

Next came the slow walk through the long, cupboard-lined hallway that led into the dining room. It was fun to drag my hand along as I counted each door. Then we crossed the room to a door that hid the stairway, and we climbed to the magical bedroom.

Sandwiched between the goose-down comforters, we felt cozy and secure, ready to sleep the night away and wake to the smells of maple syrup and buckwheat pancakes. Breakfast on the farm was always fun, and there were always fried potatoes and ham or sausage.

After breakfast, it was time to make the rounds to kiss everyone goodbye. During the long ride home, Mom and Dad chatted about what this one and that one had said. I interrupted: "When can we go back to the farm?" ❖

Then There Was Sunday!

By Marianna K. Tull

In some ways, when I was growing up back in the 1930s, Sundays were no different from school days. The most glaring similarity was the time of morning I had to drag my little body out of bed! No matter what day it was, I had to get up early enough to make my bed before I went downstairs to eat breakfast.

My mother expected my brother and me to sit down at the table with her and my father so he could say the blessing. In cold weather there was no escape from the Wheatena, Cream of Wheat or Rolled Oats—all of which I hated with a passion. Summer was *my* time of year—I could enjoy a bowl of cornflakes or puffed rice. Sometimes my mother would treat us to homemade doughnuts or cinnamon buns instead of the regular toast and homemade apple butter.

Before we put on the last of our Sunday-go-to-meetin' clothes, there were dishes to be washed and dried. I was usually the dryer. My mother always accused me of developing a "dishwashing stomachache" so I could run upstairs to finish getting dressed.

Sunday meant white cotton stockings and black patent-leather strap pumps instead of the everyday brown cotton stockings and Buster Browns. There was no "dilly-dallying" because my mother taught the ladies' Bible class, and heaven forbid she be late! At a top speed of 25 miles an hour, it took time to cover the three miles to the church. If it was cold or rainy, our Model T touring car had to be reinforced with isinglass curtains and supplied with blankets.

Our minister was a very personable young man who was attending ministerial school in Delaware. He practiced on our congregation since we did not have a permanent pastor. As one of her contributions to her church, my mother agreed to give the minister Sunday dinner. He just didn't know how lucky he was. My mother was a superb cook and baker. (Whenever her Sunday-school class had a bake sale, her cinnamon kuchens never made it to the sale; they were all sold beforehand.)

You can really be polite when the minister is across from you. My father always asked him to say the blessing. It was even longer than my father's—and we were hungry! After dinner, the minister usually made calls on members of the congregation.

> *You can really be polite when the minister is across from you.*

It wasn't too often that I plagued my mother with "I'm bored—there's nothing to do" on Sunday. I lived on a 75-acre farm. Our yard alone included a couple of those acres, and we had two dogs, two cats, a huge barn with two full haymows, a treehouse, a bicycle, all kinds of fruit trees hanging full of luscious things in season, a brook in the meadow, a springhouse, woods to explore, hills for sledding and skiing and, from the time I was 12, a wonderful clay tennis court in the meadow.

If it rained, there was an attic overflowing with chests and trunks full of all kinds of fascinating things, including clothes from the past, even the top hat my uncle used to wear to the opera. At one time during those early years, I was the proud mother of 27 dolls, and I had all kinds of cooking utensils and a china tea set that I loved to arrange on the round walnut tea table my father had made for me one Christmas.

Sunday afternoons were always full of fun—but then came the evening. If I had not been industrious on Friday night or Saturday, homework reared its ugly head! But when it came time for my mother to tuck me in and hear my "Now I lay me," I knew it had been a good Sunday. I just didn't realize how good until I got a glimpse of the un-Sunday things today's children are exposed to! ❖

Our Sunday Best

By Helen Johnson

Whenever I hear the old song *Church in the Wildwood*, my thoughts travel back to a spot dear to my childhood: a little, *white*, wooden church in a clearing in North Texas. Shade trees surround the little church at the edge of the clearing, and a community cemetery adjoins the churchyard.

The members of our family—Mother, Dad, brother, three sisters and I—crowd into our 1932 Auburn sedan, driving slowly over country roads, because there are horseback riders, wagons and buggies, all traveling churchward.

My brother, Bill, who avidly studies cars, names the make and model of each car we see. There's a 1930 American Austin, Ford Tin Lizzies, a Model A coupe and Chevrolet roadsters. At the church parking area, horses, buggies and wagons line one end while cars line the other three sides.

We're dressed in our Sunday best; Mother and my older sisters are good seamstresses. For Sunday, they made me a Shirley Temple–style dress with a short, pleated skirt. Altered hand-me-downs will do for every other day, but not Sunday. My mother wears a dark, long-sleeved dress of midcalf length, as do my sisters. Lola, my oldest sister, proudly wears a fitted beret and carries a clutch bag. The men of our farming community who attend church wear a motley selection of clothing, from suits to shirts, pants and suspenders, to overalls. Anything seems acceptable for the men!

Inside, pews without benefit of cushions stand in the center of the room. An old upright piano and speaker's stand face the pews. Usually a seminary student from Fort Worth preaches, and Mother plays piano. We sing old hymns such as *On Jordan's Stormy Banks, Sweet By and By* and *When the Roll Is Called Up Yonder.*

In the corners of one room are chairs for Sunday school classes: adult, young people, children and preschool. Our preschool chairs were made from apple boxes and trimmed with ruffles of blue-flowered material. I eagerly receive the picture Bible-story leaflet each week; Mother reads it to me again at home.

When adult meetings are long, we are allowed to go outside. Our favorite pastime is walking around in the cemetery; Bill reads aloud the names on headstones. My grandfather, grandmother and Aunt Lena are buried here.

In the spring, on the Saturday before Decoration Day, families come for cemetery cleanup. Children are allowed to play instead of "helping," so we have an exciting time.

Early on Decoration Day, Mother is in her rose garden, cutting red, pink, yellow and white roses for bouquets for family graves. After the service, there is "dinner on the ground" under the trees. Also, there's fried chicken, potato salad, baked beans and cake. After our community picnic under the trees, we're allowed to play games like hide-and-seek and red rover.

There were happy times and sad times in the little church: weddings and funerals. Our early days were mostly happy and carefree, and the "little *white* church in the wildwood" played a central part in those happy times. It was indeed "dear to my childhood."

Now, years have come and gone; families, including ours, have moved away from the community. But my thoughts sometimes return to that simpler time and the place where our family worshiped together and shared the joys and sorrows of community life. ❖

Altered hand-me-downs will do for every other day, but not for Sunday.

The Acorn Bank

By Janet Lee Friesorger

*L*et's all fill our acorn banks to help the missionaries!" our Sunday school director urged. Every year, our church distributed ceramic acorn banks with a shiny brown glaze to all the children. We felt so special to be participating. We were to put as many pennies as we could in the banks. Then, on a specified date, we would march to the front of the church and smash our banks with a hammer. All the money would be gathered up and sent to the missionaries. That was the plan, anyway.

With the enthusiasm only a 5-year-old can muster, I brought home my bank and began depositing pennies. As time dragged on, however, I became impatient with the whole process.

I shook the bank vigorously, and it still sounded almost empty! Soon my inventive little brain came up with a way to "beat the system." When Mother wasn't looking, I dropped in other small objects, like buttons and hairpins. I was proud of the rapid rate at which my acorn was being filled. Nobody noticed my secret deposits. I lived in self-satisfied bliss for a season.

But the moment of truth finally arrived. We carried our acorns to church, and the time came for me to advance to the front and smash my bank. Suddenly, I realized that my sin was "about to find me out." I began to cry and refused to walk to the front. My perplexed mother muttered something about how shy I was becoming, and arranged for a boy in my class to break the bank for me.

"Mischievous Mike" Bickham was more than happy to oblige. He *loved* to break stuff! He often spent his Sunday school time teasing me, but today he was on his best behavior, thrilled to be in the spotlight for *two* bank-breakings. Meanwhile, one very uncomfortable little girl wished she could be someplace else. All my wishing proved to be futile, however.

I don't remember the actual moment of reckoning, but I *do* remember my mother's extreme

*A*corn Bank Breaking Services are still very much alive at the First Missionary Church in Berne, Ind. Max Haines, pastor at the church, provided the ceramic acorn bank pictured above, which is very similar to the one the author remembers.

This bank is from the 1960s and is part of his personal collection.

These days, the church uses plastic acorn banks, but the kids still greatly enjoy breaking their banks, filled with their own money.

The banks are placed in plastic bags and the children break them with a hammer. Church volunteers then gather all the money amidst broken pieces.

The money collected from the banks goes to children of missionaries. Afterwards, each child receives a new acorn bank to start saving for the next year's Acorn Bank Breaking Service. ❖

embarrassment as the Sunday school superintendent quietly handed her a bag with my "treasures" inside. I remember being interrogated all the way home: "What were you thinking? Whatever possessed you to *do* that?" In following years, the church continued to use acorn banks, but I never repeated my "crime."

I learned more from that event than from all the lessons they tried to teach me at Sunday school. I discovered that experience (although unpleasant) can be a very effective teacher.

Realization dawned that all those verses I had learned to recite were not just words. They were *true*! The hidden *had* been revealed, my sin *had* found me out. I learned that God could see me even when Mother wasn't looking! But best of all, I found out that He still loved me in spite of my perverse nature.

I was repentant. All was forgiven, and I could continue to participate in the missionary offering in the years to come. ❖

Bringing in the Sheaves

By Louise Mattox

As we neared the little Baptist church in a very small town in northeastern Oklahoma, we heard the children and elders singing *Bringing in the Sheaves*. We were late, perhaps by 10 minutes, as the dirt road from our farm six miles in the country was muddy and almost impassable. It had rained almost all night, so the mud was thick and deep.

My father had hitched up Dan and Q, a matched pair of white horses that had taken prizes in pulling contests over the years. They pulled our two-seated buggy. Mother and Dad sat in the front seat, and we three girls sat in the back. When it was cold or windy, Mother would tie a thin silk scarf over our faces so we wouldn't get windburned. Only one scarf was white and could be seen through, and we had to take turns wearing it. Mother would also heat bricks to keep our feet warm.

"Bringing in the sheaves," we began to sing as we took our seats in the last row of pews.

Mother was a strong believer in gathering sheaves. She started a boys' Sunday-school class for young men ages 12–15. It enjoyed very good attendance, probably because she had organized two baseball teams, the Royal Ambassadors and the King's Men. The teams played each other, other teams from town and teams from neighboring towns. Mother had been the

only girl among five brothers, so she had direct knowledge as to what interested boys. The class grew and grew!

Our small town had no library, no art center, no amusement park and no swimming pool, so the two churches were very important in the life of the small community.

Not only did they meet spiritual needs, but they fulfilled recreational needs also. It was not uncommon to have potluck suppers, pie socials, spelling bees, musicals, debates, parties (especially at Halloween and Christmas) and ballgames in the vacant lot in back of the church.

Often the church exchanged services with the church from the all-black town of Melvin. How their congregation could sing! And the suppers were great—I especially enjoyed the fried pies.

When we had a baseball game, the men covered the windows with screen wire to protect them from any well-hit ball. When entertainment was in the offing, one could hear up and down Main Street, "Is that doings at the Methodist or Baptist tonight?"

I wonder what happened to all the little "sheaves"? I know that one became a minister and was doing his share to bring in the sheaves, but there were others. All now would be in their 80s or even 90s, and many are no doubt among the harvest in the sky. Amen! ❖

Just As I Am

By Dorothy Peterson

*J*udy walked slowly into the Fruitvale Community Church that special morning in the summer of 1946, as the congregation was singing *Just as I Am.* It was an old familiar hymn that Judy heard most every Sunday morning. She lived near the church, just walking distance, and decided she would like to visit the place of worship, where *Just as I Am* was sung every week. She knew the minister's family, and the opportunity was just right for her visit.

The doors of the little church were left open because it was a hot day in Fruitvale, Calif., 10 miles north of Bakersfield.

Judy walked slowly up the aisle and paused at each row until she recognized the minister's wife, seated in the front row of the church. She continued to proudly walk up to the front of the church and then sat herself next to the minister's wife, who smiled with a faint expression of embarrassment. Judy held her head high and, wearing her only coat, set her dignified tail down and looked up at the minister.

> ### *Judy walked slowly up the aisle and paused at each row.*

The minister, viewing the humor unfolding before his eyes, kept leading the congregation in *Just as I Am.*

My brother Marvin and I were choir members, and watching Judy sit there, looking at the song-leading minister, we tried to stifle giggles and laughter.

That laughter got much louder when the minister started laughing himself, pausing only to catch his breath as he sang *Just as I Am.*

In another second, laughter caused the minister's new dentures to explode into orbit, out of his mouth and over the pulpit.

His maneuvers as he tried to catch his teeth, and Judy trying to catch a visit to church, made for a day I will always remember.

Judy, you see, was our beloved dog. The minister and his wife were Papa and Mama. Our home was directly behind the church. Someone left our gate open, and Judy walked right into church.

The hymn *Just as I Am* must have made my dad feel the real truth of that song, when he lost his new dentures and a strange four footed friend came to church.

Sometimes I would sing *Just as I Am* while washing the dishes. Judy would sit and listen and wag her tail as I cleaned off the plates. I wonder if the hymn brought back memories of her visit to church or if she was just hungry. ❖

Sundays Were Special

By Alice Swope

*I*n the 1930s, in my childhood home on the outskirts of a little town in eastern Montana, Sundays were very special. During the week, my two brothers and I had chores to perform before we went to school. There were eggs to gather and cows to milk. Sometimes we had to feed a newborn lamb whose mother would not accept it.

But my folks were always very careful to see that our chores were not excessive, for they wanted us to have enough time to study. Getting good grades was important to them.

On Saturdays we all went to town so that my father could sell the eggs for the grand price of 50 cents for five dozen. We'd receive another $2 for the cream he took to the dairy. My brothers and I were in awe of anyone who got so much money.

Then, every Sunday after church, Dad would give each of us a nickel. We all had different plans for our money, and our plans were always the same. My brother Ervin would use his for a movie, and my brother Edwin would use his to purchase the *Sunday Denver Post* newspaper.

As for me, that nickel would burn a hole in my pocket all week. I'd look at it and rub it between my thumb and fingers as I thought about the next Sunday, when I'd get another nickel, making it possible for me to enjoy my special pleasure: a big, delicious, strawberry ice-cream soda. Shutting my eyes, I could feel myself sitting on that small, round stool in the local drugstore, sipping my special treat through a straw. Licking my lips, I could almost taste the wonderful, creamy soda.

Staying Warm by the Stove by Charles Berger, House of White Birches nostalgia archives

On Sunday evenings, after the dinner dishes were put away, we'd sit in our favorite chairs in the living room and wait for the fun to begin. Mom would bring out her mending basket, and Dad would lean back with his hands behind his head, waiting for us to begin. He'd grin at us and then turn toward Ervin.

"OK, Erv, let's hear about that movie," he'd say. Ervin was very good at telling stories. Sometimes he even acted out some of the parts. After we'd enjoyed the movie, Dad would clap his hands and say, "Great job. As usual, just great. I feel as if I'd been there with you."

Then he'd look at Edwin. "So, Bud, how are the funnies this week?" The *Denver Post* was such a big newspaper with so many comic pages that we spent the evening enjoying it.

Before we went to bed, the boys would look at me and ask, "So what do *you* have to share?" I should have felt guilty because I never shared my 10 cents. But the memory of the soda's sweet, cool taste was enough to wipe away any guilt. My brothers couldn't hold it against me. They knew we all spent our money on things that were special to each of us.

Years later, when we had enough money that we could all go to the movies together or sit in that drugstore enjoying our favorite sodas, it was never quite the same. While it was wonderful to have the whole family participate, the anticipation and excitement were gone.

I've got to admit that I still love those big sodas, although I've found very few places that serve them anymore. I'd love to find an old-fashioned drugstore with an old-fashioned soda fountain like they had in the '30s. ❖

Sunday With the Mayor

By Madeline J. Dent Huss

On Sunday mornings in the mid-1930s, New York City Mayor Fiorello LaGuardia read the comics to his young audience on his radio program. Fortunately, our small town in New Jersey could pick up the mayor's broadcast. We'd spread out our Sunday paper on the floor and wait for his program to come on.

We sprawled out on our stomachs, anxious for the program to begin. It was more fun reading the funnies with the mayor than reading them on our own. Enthralled, we listened and read the four pages of comics. *The Katzenjammer Kids*, *Maggie and Jiggs*, and *Barney Google* were our favorites.

We followed their adventures faithfully; missing a week was absolutely unthinkable.

One Sunday I scrambled up during an commercial to get a glass of water, stumbled and fell on the fan-shaped mesh speaker and flattened it. The mayor's voice sputtered and was silent.

Mom rushed in from the kitchen. "Oh no, there goes the radio!" She helped me to my feet. "I warned you about being careful."

I burst into tears.

"No use crying over spilled milk," Mom said. "We'll have to learn to do without the radio until we can save up to buy a new one."

I was given no punishment. It was enough to know that I had deprived the entire family of listening to the radio for several weeks. We especially missed our Sunday-morning treat of listening to the mayor reading the funnies. ❖

The Katzenjammer Kids © 1938, Licensed by King Features

Toots and Casper

By Jimmy Murphy

Sunday Drives and Spotted Fawns

By Dale Simmons

*I*f you grew up in rural Saskatchewan during the 1950s, you'll be familiar with a tradition called "the Sunday drive." And if you weren't privileged to participate in it, then you have indeed missed out on something special. Saskatchewan winters are long and hard, and when I was a kid, the cold weather kept us pretty close to home. I got to school every day, weather permitting.

And we went to town at least once a week to do the shopping and collect the mail; we also visited neighbors and they called on us. But excursions any farther afield were well-nigh impossible. As a result, when winter finally released its grip on the prairies and the roads again became passable, we were more than ready to venture forth.

Sundays were a day of rest for us. No matter how good the weather, and no matter how great the temptation to do field work, Sunday was the Lord's day, and even if we didn't attend church, we honored Him by abstaining from labor.

Lord's day or not, there were chores to be done; Dad called them essentials.

So how did we spend our warm-weather Sundays? Well, like I said, we'd go for a drive.

We owned a number of automobiles when I was a kid, but the one I remember most vividly—and the one I liked best—was our 1952 Pontiac. It was high and wide, and it was handsome. It was light gray with a matching interior. The firm, comfortable seats were covered in a plush material with a soft nap, and when I ran my hands over it, it tickled my palms. And most importantly, it had a radio. This meant that on summer Sundays when baseball games were broadcast, Dad could catch the action while chauffeuring us around the countryside.

Like every other day of the week, Sundays began early. Lord's day or not, there were chores to be done; Dad called them "essentials." Cows had to be milked, the milk separated, and eggs gathered. But once these details were taken care of, the day was ours.

Our Sunday drives followed a pattern. It was the unexpected events and the little adventures that made each excursion unique. For instance:

I was 10 years old, so that would make it the summer of 1952, the year we got the Pontiac. It must have been getting on toward mid-August because the grain was beginning to ripen. After doing chores and having a bit of lunch, we changed from work clothes to something less casual and got ready to go for a drive.

Mom always put together a picnic: a thermos of coffee for her and Dad, bottled drinks for me, some fresh fruit, hard-boiled eggs and baking-powder biscuits. Nothing fancy, but real easy on the palate. And then, while Dad went to fetch the car, Mom and I would wait in the driveway beside the house.

Our garage was next to the barn, so Dad had a ways to go. And the wait for him to get back only heightened my anticipation. I can still envision that beautiful gray automobile rounding the

This 1952 Pontiac Chieftain is like the one the author's family took on those Sunday drives. Photo courtesy House of White Birches nostalgia archives.

corner at the end of the lane, and easing majestically to a halt in front of us.

Mom always rode up front with Dad, and I didn't mind a bit. It meant I had the backseat all to myself.

On this particular day, we drove south of town. Dad had it in mind to check the crops on the farms that bordered the Qu'Appelle Valley. I especially liked this area. Deep coulees fingered their way from the parent valley, reaching far into farm country, and I knew that with a little coaxing, Dad could be persuaded to stop awhile and let me go exploring.

We were on the road by 1 o'clock. We followed the main road leading south of Balcarres for a couple of miles, then Dad steered us onto the grid roads that crisscrossed the region.

The key to a good Sunday drive was the pace, and for us, the average pace was *slow*. Ten miles an hour was considered fast; 5 miles an

hour was about right. Why so slow? We wanted to see everything we drove past. And what were we looking for? Well, that depended on who you were. Dad was interested in the crops that grew in the roadside fields. Mom's attention was directed more toward the farm yards we passed, and the state of lawns, flower beds and gardens.

Mom also kept an eye peeled for berry patches. In those days, wild fruit was more commonly consumed than the domestic kind. And these outings helped pinpoint where to find saskatoons and raspberries when they ripened early in the season, and where to locate chokecherries and pin cherries later in the summer. The key was spotting the blossoms, then making a mental note of where they'd been seen, so we could return and do the harvesting. It may sound simple enough, but it was a feat that took a sharp eye and a keen memory. And my mother possessed both.

What did I watch for? Well, that varied, and sometimes from minute to minute. I was a bird-watcher and kept a list, so I was always looking for new species to add to the tally. And I'll never forget the day I spotted my first lark bunting: a stunning little black-and-white bird, perched on a droopy strand of barbed wire.

I also kept an eye out for beer or pop bottles that had been discarded in the ditch. Dad would stop so I could pick them up. It was a great way to supplement my allowance.

Whenever we encountered farmers working near the road, Dad would stop to talk, and they never hesitated to shut their tractors down and visit awhile. While they were engaged in crop talk, I'd go exploring. If poplar bluffs were nearby, I'd check them for the antlers male deer discarded every spring. And if there was a summer-fallow field handy, I'd check any wind-swept areas for arrowheads. When it was time to proceed, Dad would beep the horn as a signal for me to return to the car.

Around 2 o'clock in the afternoon, we'd stop for lunch. Dad would park in the shade of a poplar bluff, and we'd haul the picnic basket out of the trunk. For an hour we'd snack and relax, or at least Mom and Dad would.

I'd eat as quickly as good manners would allow and then set off to do some scouting. I remember many such stops and many such meals, but one in particular stands out.

We were near the rim of the Qu'Appelle Valley. Dad had parked on an approach that gave access to a stretch of unfenced pasture. After a hurried sandwich, I grabbed an apple and set off to see what I could find. And on this day, I found something special.

Near the middle of the pasture grew a mixed stand of scrub poplar and saskatoon bushes. The berries growing where the sun could get at them were almost ripe, and "almost ripe" was good enough for me. I was picking the fruit and eating it, and while concentrating on reaching the best berries, I wasn't watching where I was putting my feet. As a result, I nearly stepped on the prettiest little spotted fawn I'd ever seen.

The young whitetail couldn't have been more than three or four days old. He'd obviously been left there by his mother while she fed or went for water. She'd was certainly close by, watching and worried for the safety of her fawn.

For a moment I froze, staring down at the baby deer. He had his eyes fixed on me. I backed off a couple of steps, and then got down on one knee. Less than 6 feet separated us. I'd never been so close to a fawn. I don't know how long we studied each other. I lost track of time. The soft wind fingering its way through the trees overhead made the only sound. The sunlight filtering through the leaves struck the fawn's coat, creating the illusion that his spots were dancing. It was almost magical.

When Dad beeped the horn, both the fawn and I were startled. I jumped, and he flattened out in the grass. I backed away from him until I lost sight of him in the undergrowth. Then I headed for the car, confident that the fawn's mother would return to comfort her offspring.

I was bursting to tell my parents what I'd seen. They seemed suitably impressed. Then Dad drew my attention to something I'd been too excited to notice. This fawn had been born late. Most young of the year had already begun to shed their spots, while this little guy had barely grown his. He'd have to mature quickly, and rely on his wits to make it through the winter. I was sure he would. He looked smart.

After lunch we'd resume travel, and in the afternoon we'd often stop in at the farm yards and visit there. Mom got to talk with friends she didn't often see. After participating in enough conversation to be polite, Dad and I would drift away to look around the barn and stock pens.

Evaluating a neighbor's livestock wasn't just a matter of satisfying idle curiosity. We were always looking to improve the bloodlines of our own stock, and if someone else had superior-looking animals, we were always anxious to find out how the new strains got into the area, and whether or not we could access them.

It wasn't just the state of grain crops we checked on, either. Dad would pull over to monitor the quality of hay grown in meadows. The condition of pastureland also came under scrutiny, as did the degree of moisture to be found in summer-fallow fields.

The journey seldom took us more than 10 miles from home, and on the way back, Dad would follow a different route just to vary the scenery. Summer evenings on the prairies are long. The sun lingers above the horizon until after 9 o'clock, and we knew we'd have plenty of time to see to the evening chores.

Back home, Dad would drop Mom and me off at the house and then proceed to the implement shed. I'd change into everyday clothes and go join him. Dad never once simply put the car away. Every time he drove it into shelter, he'd check the oil and the radiator; he'd clean the windshield and wipe down the chrome. It's no wonder our vehicles lasted so long; they were pampered like members of the family. Then once Dad had also changed clothes, we'd see to the chores and have some supper.

Those days and our Sunday drives are now things of the past. But my memories of the occasion are still vital.

I remember seeing my dad standing chest-deep in a field of ripening grain. I remember the perfumed scent of new-mown hay, and the clean smell of freshly turned summer-fallow. And I remember standing in a poplar bluff, listening intently as a fitful breeze crept through the leaves overhead. I remember curling up on the backseat on the way home from our drives, feeling warm and secure.

And I remember a spotted fawn. ❖

Going for a Drive

By Ginger K. Nelson

The sign in front of the gas pump says $2.81, $2.91, $3.01! By the time you read this, the prices may have gone up even higher. What were they in 1945? I don't remember, but they must have been a great deal lower, because it seemed we were always "going for a drive" on a Sunday afternoon.

1932 Essex ad, House of White Birches nostalgia archives

There were pine-covered mountains and grass-green valleys to see. Red cardinals flitted through budding foliage all around us. There were few road signs along unmarked highways, but plenty of room to turn around if we got lost, which we inevitably did.

We gazed at the bend of the small sycamore trees. We stared at the rickety wooden cabins, which often housed folks in overalls with dirty, old handkerchiefs. We waved to the campers who sat beside their trailers in the middle of nowhere.

At the end of gazing, staring and waving, we often dozed in the large backseat on our way home while the grown-ups sang the latest songs and used the recent slang.

All of it trailed through our minds as sleep overtook us, rocking us with the rhythms of the songs and the swaying of the car as it rounded homeward bends in the road.

Halting at a roadside inn near our town, we smeared mustard and catsup over steaming hot dogs, poked straws into strawberry milkshakes, and munched French fries dripping in salted grease. Sleep long ago wiped from our eyes, we watched carhops skate between the cars, wielding trays with food. What wonderful music blared over the speakers from the indoor booths that sported individual jukeboxes! Frank Sinatra, Bing Crosby, the Andrews Sisters, and the sounds of the Big Bands promised us eternal love or sang sad songs of unrequited love.

Finally we headed for home, our weekly drive nearly over. Our suburban streets spread granite-colored in front of us, dotted with half-melted lines of tar, honeysuckle sneaking through sticky bushes. Houses with no garages, no fences, and no sidewalks greeted us, as did the other boys and girls dotting the streets, wielding homemade bats and rubber band–covered balls. "Can you play?" voices echoed.

Fatigue forgotten, we jumped from our car and eagerly joined them. "Who's up next?"

Sunday drives from the past … when gas prices didn't threaten, when children enjoyed excursions but liked coming home better, and when memories built up like dips of ice-cream cones reaching toward the sky.

Weren't they wonderful? ❖

The Sunday Ride

By John Dinan

*I*n the 1940s, the city was a pretty complete place. Within walking distance we could get our groceries, and a short bus ride took us downtown where we could satisfy all our remaining shopping needs.

On Sundays we walked to church, looking forward to one of Mother's great dinners at noon. Then, as Sunday afternoon dragged on, my sister would put the pressure on my father to fire up the Oldsmobile and "take a ride."

My father didn't need much encouragement. He and my mother would sit up front, and my sister and I would sit in the backseat. Around the outskirts of the city, our ride took us along the road that followed the beach and out to Route 1, which went north to New Hampshire and eventually to Maine.

These rides were a treat, especially when the country took on the beautiful colors of fall. Trees and farm buildings and horses and other sights unfamiliar to the city dweller beckoned.

There was one feature of Route 1 that I always watched for. At the top of a hill, slanted mirrors were positioned on crosspieces over the highway, allowing approaching motorists to see what was coming up the other side. I guess they hadn't thought of the yellow line dividers.

One of our stops on these rides was at Dodge's, an ice-cream stand that had a special milkshake offer. The milkshakes were very large, and Dodge's advertised that if you could drink five and live, you wouldn't have to pay. In all the years they were in business, I only heard of one person collecting on the offer.

Soon enough it was time to return to our home in the city. As I remembered it, the time factor here was determined by how long it would take to get home, eat and settle in for the evening radio offering of *The Shadow*.

Car rides today are taken almost exclusively out of necessity. If someone suggested taking a ride for its own sake today, he'd be looked at with wonderment. ❖

1947 Nash ad, House of White Birches nostalgia archives

Weekend Drives In the '30s

By Richard Jackson

After church, and after a dinner of roast, potatoes, gravy and cake, what was there to do on a Sunday afternoon back then when we were kids? Couldn't play ball, couldn't ride the bike, and the stores were closed. It was Sunday, and it was different. There was no television in the 1930s, and the radio didn't come on until 7 p.m., in time for Jack Benny.

What did we do? In our family, as in many, we went for a afternoon ride. Get the Ford out, and away we would go. Maybe not too far; maybe clear to Pittsburgh—about 30 miles! The distance and the time were usually regulated by needing to be at Grandma's in time for supper (6 o'clock; set your watch by it).

The roads were a little narrower, the curves curvier and the hills steeper, so speed usually was not a problem. At 35–45 miles per hour, it was easier to look around, see all the interesting sights and wave at friends. I once saw the Ford's speedometer reach 50, and I was amazed. When I told my dad that my mother had done that, he questioned the necessity of taking chances on the highway.

Cars were a lot different then—a lot less comfortable than today's and a little more difficult to drive, too, since the driver had to shift gears; there were no automatics. In the hilly country where I grew up, there was a lot of gear shifting. A flat stretch there was one where you could go two blocks without shifting out of high gear.

In the summertime the "air conditioning" was the open window plus some side vents. Car engines overheated more then, and we often saw cars pulled off the road with steam pouring out of the radiators.

In the '30s, there were no heaters in cars, so it really got cold. Everyone kept blankets or lap robes in their cars. We had one we called the Indian blanket, and was it ever scratchy! But it was warm. We were glad when the late '40s came along and brought more comfortable cars.

Flat tires were common. Everyone had to learn how to change a flat.

Back when we drove our Model A, if it rained, there was only one windshield wiper. In some cars it had to be operated by hand—another duty for the driver. There were no turn signals, either, so the driver had to stick his arm out the window and point.

Many cars did not have trunks, so there were folding racks that fit on the running board. That is where the suitcases or picnic baskets went. Then we hoped it didn't rain.

Flat tires were quite common. That didn't change when the late '40s came along. The roads weren't all that good, nor were the tires. Everyone had to learn how to change a flat.

Speaking of tires, there were no snow tires then, but there were chains. But people didn't put their chains on and ride around on the bare pavement. Nope, they went on after it snowed, which meant getting cold and wet getting them on properly.

In spite of all that, those experiences were fun—and still are, as many of us continue the custom. I still like to recall those days when we chugged along at 35 miles per hour with the wind in our faces and read those Burma Shave signs on the Sunday-afternoon drive. ❖

A Ride With Daddy

By Virginia M. Baty

As children, my three sisters and one brother and I didn't see our daddy much during the week. During the late 1940s, he worked at night driving a city bus, and we attended school during the day. But on Sundays, he really made up for lost time.

And how we looked forward to Sundays! Daddy would begin the day by fixing us a scrumptious breakfast of fried potatoes and eggs, juice, and delicious, hot, cinnamon rolls that Mama had made. We had Bible reading and prayer, and then attended church together.

After church, we enjoyed one of Mother's delicious dinners of roast beef, mashed potatoes and gravy with all the trimmings. Afterward we took a short rest, knowing that Daddy would take us for a ride in the country when we awakened. If we stirred before Daddy, we would walk on tiptoe until he got up. We looked forward to that ride more than anything!

Since Daddy had lived in the same part of Nebraska his entire life, we experienced a different area of the country each week. We usually drove to places he had visited as a boy. He would make our ride more interesting by telling us exciting stories as we rode along.

There was the time he and his brothers fished in "that creek," or when they flew down "Jack Rabbit Hill" on their sleds. This hill was very steep, and as we flew down it in the car, we could almost imagine that we were on our sleds with the wind in our faces. What fun!

Sometimes Daddy parked the car so we could walk to the railroad tracks. He pointed out the first railroad was made with wooden rails and steel spikes. He also reminded us that the

The author's father in 1954.

windmills we saw produced water for the farmers. Daddy showed us the fields of corn, wheat and alfalfa and explained that the combines we saw in the fields would cut and separate grain from chaff. We would see large haystacks, wildflowers, milkweed pods and cattails. Mother loved cattails, and we often stopped to pick a bouquet for her.

As we rode along, Daddy showed us how to recognize the tracks of rabbits and squirrels as they scampered along. He taught us the different kinds of cows and how to know each by its appearance—spotted, black, brown, etc.

Daddy knew the names of the trees, birds and butterflies we saw, too. There were large trees he remembered climbing as a boy with his friends. He told us all about their adventures in the woods where they played hide-and-seek. He made it seem so real that we felt that we had been part of the game.

Many times Daddy took us to the zoo as we headed home. We loved the zoo and all the animals, especially the monkeys. Daddy would make animal sounds at them, and they would mimic him as they jumped from place to place.

The zoo was near a rose garden called The Sunken Garden. In the center of it was a duck pond. We often took bread to feed the ducks.

Other times, Daddy would drive us to the roundhouse where the railroad engines switched cars. It was like watching a giant puzzle as the cars moved from one set of tracks to another. We often wondered how they could do it with such precision and not run into each other.

We never tired of taking rides with Daddy. It is still the most enjoyable childhood memory we have. Will we ever forget those rides with Daddy? *Never!* ❖

Chicken Sunday

By Charlotte Ann Trent
as told to Donna McGuire Tanner

When I was growing up, I lived with my grandmother, Viola Trent, in the small community of Weirwood, W.Va. She always made sure that she had plenty for me to eat on our daily table, but meat was rarely served. So it was a great delight for me when "Chicken Sunday" rolled around.

Once a month, my Aunt Ruth, Uncle Roy and their children, Sheila, Gary, Gregory, twins Harold and Darrell, and Debbie, traveled a distance from their home in Oceana, W.Va., for Sunday supper.

After church—we never missed Sunday services—Grandma would go to the section of the yard where we kept our chickens to fetch two of them. Their destiny was to be our supper.

When the car came up the dirt road and stopped at Grandma's house, I would race down to greet them. My aunt and uncle owned Trent's Market, a grocery store. I knew that they would be carrying a large box full of groceries, including foods that we usually could not buy for ourselves. I can still see the bunch of ripe bananas lying on the top.

In warm weather, my cousins and I would play games out in the yard while Grandma and Aunt Ruth prepared the meal. Fried chicken was usually the main course, but some Sundays, Grandma served chicken and dumplings, another of her specialties.

Sometimes I would linger in the kitchen just to watch Grandma prepare the dumplings. She would mix and roll out the dumpling dough. Then she would slice it into long strips before dropping each piece into the piping-hot chicken broth with chicken breasts divided into four or six pieces, depending on how large the chicken had been.

It was a great delight for me when "Chicken Sunday" rolled around.

In the summer, Grandma would gather from her vegetable garden fresh green beans, new potatoes, roasting ears of corn on the cob, tomatoes and cucumbers. She would make coleslaw using fresh peppers, onions and tomatoes, and mixed with her special salad dressing. In the winter months, we feasted on home-canned vegetables.

Chocolate pie was always the dessert. My grandmother would beat two egg yolks until they were airy. Then she would add sugar that had been blended with cocoa powder. After these ingredients had been mixed well, she would add milk. This mixture was poured into her homemade pie shell. Next she would pop it into the oven of the wood-burning stove. I can still almost taste that dreamy delight.

While we children played, our stomachs growled as the aromas of the Sunday meal reached our nostrils. It was traditional with most families in the area that the children were fed last, after the adults had finished. Looking back, it surprises me that there was always enough food for all of us. I still wonder how Grandma managed to do it.

Toward the end of the day, Grandma had a special treat for us kids. She gave each of us one of her homemade chocolate "popsicles," which she had mixed and frozen the previous day.

After supper, we would often sit on the porch. Grandma would gather her grandchildren around her. She would scrape an apple with a case knife and feed it to us. We children relished this treat and our time with her.

My Aunt Ruth and I often reminisce about this time in our lives. She will say, "No one could make chocolate pies like your Grandma." As we remember, we conjure up visions of the day we call "Chicken Sunday." ❖

I Was a Hungry Kid

By M.E. Smith

Whenever Mother and I visited Grandma and Cousin Thelma, Sunday dinner was always late—and I was hungry long before it was ready. It was the early 1930s and we were living in Moran, Kansas. I had no playmates, no radio, no television, no pets—nothing to distract me from my hunger.

While the cooking—and talking—was going on, I was on my own to forage. Today when we hike in the woods, my wife criticizes my penchant for nibbling on plants and berries; maybe I picked up that habit while waiting for dinner at Grandma's. I nibbled on shepherd's purse and wood sorrel in her yard and on purslane from the bare ground that once had been the garden. But I dared not try the mushrooms because Mother said most were poisonous.

However, in season, there was enough fruit to satisfy. In spring there were delicious mulberries. In the fall, a pear tree produced exceptionally good pears. Mother ate pears from that tree in 1908; in 1990, I was saddened to find that the old tree had been cut down. It had been my custom to stop for a few pears whenever I visited my parents' and Grandma's graves nearby. If the old house was occupied, I would knock and ask for a few; otherwise, I just helped myself.

1947 Welch's ad, House of White Birches nostalgia archives

But best of all, in late summer, Grandma's Concord grape arbor offered a treat we did not have at home. I squeezed the pulp into my mouth, separated the seeds with my teeth and tongue, spit out the seeds, squeezed the juice from the skins against my teeth, and reached for another. Long before dinner, my tongue and lips were sore and my mouth blue. But my wait had been a pleasure.

Wintertime was a problem. It was chilly outside, and there was nothing edible out there anyway. So I wandered around the house, the kitchen and the pantry, exhorting the cooks to speed things up. Mother was strictly averse to my raiding the cookie jar to "spoil my dinner." I never said anything, but I wondered what use dinner would be if I didn't survive until then.

One winter Sunday afternoon in 1932, while preoccupied with my complaining stomach, I wandered into the pantry. A big, clear, glass jar sat on a shelf at eye level; there was a big tablespoon in it, and no one was watching. I contemplated taking a big bite of that sugar.

I had never tasted straight sugar, but Dad often sprinkled sugar on his bread and butter. I knew that sugar was food, and that candy had a lot of sugar in it; maybe this would pacify my lonely innards.

My conscience nagged me, though. I'd been taught never to eat out of anything except my own plate or bowl, and I knew my moist mouth would make the sugar stick to the spoon and be evidence against me. But sufficient hunger produces criminals and makes one take risks. I deposited a heaping tablespoonful into my mouth, then carefully withdrew the spoon between my lips, trying to wipe it dry as I did so. Then an awful revelation came to me. It wasn't sugar! It was salt!

Ever have a mouthful of salt? It is awful! I needed to eject it fast, but I didn't want to get caught and suffer a switching when I got home. As saliva welled up in my mouth, I tried to look nonchalant. I kept my lips shut tight to avoid drooling and sneaked outside. Fortunately, there was a water hydrant, and I rinsed my mouth again and again to relieve it.

That didn't fill my stomach, but it sure took my mind off it! ❖

Sunday Fudge

By Carol Beach York

For my sister, Gloria, and me, fudge making on Sunday afternoon was a treat. In the Depression of the 1930s, our ingredients didn't include butter, vanilla or chopped nuts. We were happy if we had cocoa, sugar and milk and if Mother said we could make fudge!

We hung over the dark, bubbling pot with great anticipation. Long before the fudge was finished, we began dropping sample spoonfuls into a cup of cold water. When the fudge was done, the sample formed a soft ball in the water. Otherwise it disintegrated.

I suppose we would have ended up with a lot more fudge had we not kept testing it, but we had a wonderful time.

When we decided that the fudge was ready, we took the pot off the stove and set it in a pan of cold water. Then my sister and I took turns beating the fudge with a big spoon. The instructions were: "Beat until glossy." We weren't exactly sure what "glossy" should look like. When we tired of beating, we poured it onto a plate and watched to see if it would harden.

Sometimes it was fudge, and we could cut it into pieces and proudly show our mother. But sometimes, due to our impatience, it just lay there on the plate like thick chocolate syrup. In spite of encouraging pokes with our fingers, it remained soft and gooey. We did not often have money for ice in the icebox, but in the winter we could put our plate of gooey stuff on the cold back porch to help it harden. This often worked; when it didn't, we ate our "fudge" with a spoon.

Gloria thought that porch was the answer to our problems, and she always suggested it, even on hot summer days. "Let's put it on the back porch," she would say confidently. She was a darling little sister, and I treasure my happy memories of making Sunday fudge with her. ❖